Caliber Publications Presents

The
Carpet Installation
TRAINING
HANDBOOK

First Edition

Eric Larson

Published by:
CALIBER PUBLICATIONS
1-877-480-5790

The Carpet Installation Training Handbook
Copyright © 2002 Eric M. Larson. Copyright © 1998, 1999.

Cover design & Layout: Eric M. Larson
Cover Model: Anthony C. Kach
Book design & Layout: Eric M. Larson
Editor in Chief: Dr. William G. Burns, San Antonio, TX
All photography: Eric M. Larson
Interior Illustrations: Eric M. Larson
Photo models: Anthony Kach, Jim Johnson, Pat Diewold

First Edition
First Printing, 2002

1. Home Improvement. 2. Construction. 3. Study Aid -Training Manual. I. Title.
International Standard Book Number (ISBN): 0-9673696-0-6 (pbk.)
Library of Congress Catalog Card Number: *99-096189*
Larson, Eric
Printed in the United States of America
Printed on Recycled Paper

DISCLAIMER
Caliber Publications as well as all technical advisors, claim this handbook as a general guide only and accept no responsibility or liability for following the procedures of this handbook. Federal, State and local regulations and ordinances should also be followed. Compliance with all required (OSHA) Occupational Safety and Health Administration regulations and a follow Hazardous Communications Plan.

DEDICATION

I Dedicate This Book To My Father
RONALD D LARSON
1927-1978

Technical Advisory Board

Tom Miller

Tom has been a National Board Member of The International Certified Floorcovering Installers Association (CFI). He was the Local Cedar Rapids, IA Chapter President of the CFI from 1996 - 2002.

Tom is the manager of Hanks Specialties, a distributor of floor covering supplies. He has been in the distribution business since 1990.

Tom was a floor covering installer for 8 years prior to taking a position in distribution. He has been certified through level II residential and commercial with the International Certified Floorcovering Installers Association (CFI) and is also certified by I.E. Ardex, C-Cure, Tarkett and Domco.

Dick Wessels

Dick owns a floor covering installation business in Cedar Rapids, IA (Wessels Floor Covering) and has 30 years of vast installation experience. He also previously owned a floor covering retail store for many years. He started in the floor covering business in 1973 and installs carpet, tile, vinyl, pre finished wood floors and congoleum.

Dick is a well known and sought after installer in the Cedar Rapids, IA area, he is known as an excellent installer and is highly sought after for his quality workmanship.

Dick is a Master certified installer with the International Certified Floorcovering Installers Association. He has held the position of President of the local Cedar Rapids CFI chapter. He is also Certified by Armstrong Tarkett Congoleum.

ACKNOWLEDGMENTS

I would like to thank everyone who has helped to make this book possible. To my mother's hard work typing this manuscript on a desktop at my Uncle Ed's house in California. To Uncle Ed for the use of his computer. To Bill Burns for his excellent editing skills. To my sister Melissa and her husband Jose Miguel for allowing me to live with them for nearly two months so that I could write this book. To my first carpet trainer, Don Alter, for getting me started in the business. To Dan Colson for my final training lessons before starting my business and to all of the good times we had! To Annastacia from Waterloo for giving me motivation and inspiration. To Dr. Richard Dean Burns for his editing, and for assistance. To Tony Kach and Jim Johnson for allowing me to photograph them doing their work. To all I've hired in the past and present, Vince Kral, Pat Diewald, Jeff Carens, Bill Mefford, Troy Thompson, Joey Boffelli, thanks for the good work you did for me. To my parents for their continued support and for having me as a guest in their home so that I could work on this book. To all of the carpet installers that I've associated with since starting in this business, we are all brothers, and the work wouldn't be worth it without the friends. To the technical advisory board, Tom Miller and Dick Wessels, I greatly appreciate the time you took to read the book. To every one who wrote me endorsements for the book; thank you. Thanks to many others not listed here who have helped and encouraged me in the process of writing this book. I would also like to thank those who did not assist, encourage, or support me. I developed greater will power to stick to what I'm doing, and grew stronger in the end.

TABLE OF CONTENTS

SECTION I
THE BASICS 15

First Procedure of Installation
MEASURING FOR CARPET 41

SECTION 2
THE PROCEDURES OF INSTALLATION 59

STEP ONE 61

STEP TWO 64

SECTION 3
GLUE DOWN CARPET INSTALLATION 143

SECTION 4
CARPETING STEPS 155

SECTION 5

SOME OTHER SITUATIONS

SECTION 6

NON - STRETCHABLE CARPETS

INTRODUCTION

Congratulations on purchasing the *CARPET INSTALLATION TRAINING HANDBOOK*. I originally started writing when I was in the process of hiring new help for my own business. I didn't have any intention of writing and publishing a **book**, but just to write the basic procedures of installation to make it easier for my new help to get started on the job and to save myself the endless explanations. It was such a struggle training my new help and working on the job at the same time. Every installer has had the same problem I did. You end up working yourself into the ground and earning less in the process. There had to be a better way! My hired help needed to know the procedures and terms of installation before ever setting foot on the job site.

As I wrote, the pages grew and I realized that this could be a **BOOK,** a very useful book that all installers could use to help them train their help. As the book continued to grow, so did its usefulness and later I realized, the book would be educational in libraries for anyone wanting to know information about carpet installation. There is also a need for a good book to help people that don't have the finances to hire the work done and want as professional a looking job as possible. The final use is for the person exploring the possibility of starting their own carpet installation business. They will gain a thorough understanding of the basic procedures of Installation so that they can work with a pro installer and acquire the hands on work experience necessary, to start their own business.

So what began as a *list of installation procedures,* hand written on paper, became *THE CARPET INSTALLATION TRAINING HANDBOOK* . I hope that this book will provide educational information to libraries and those exploring starting in the carpet business, I hope professional installers can stop working so hard and start doing more supervising! I hope that this book will provide a superior education for those of you just starting in the business and make the learning as fast and easy as possible and I hope that this book will help those on a tight budget to install their own carpet in a professional way.

Not only did the book grow but I grew as well, realizing that if you put your mind to something and never give up you can accomplish anything in life. I didn't own a computer when I started work on this project, nor did I know anything about using a computer. I didn't know anything about publishing or publishing software. I thought that everyone would be as enthusiastic about the project as I was, but for whatever psychological reasons some people were negative about the book and some were negative towards me personally. Although this may sound negative, it has been a positive experience for me. There is no such thing as a negative experience once you've learned and grown from the experience.

The most satisfying part of carpet installation for me is seeing the finished job and knowing it was a job well done, knowing that you are improving people's homes is very rewarding. I have also always liked the physical aspect of "putting in a hard days work" you feel good at the end of the day when you've physically exerted yourself rather than just siting at a desk all day. Carrying in carpet, tools, kicking, stretching, and trimming the carpet will keep you in better than average shape.

I am currently moving on to other adventures in my life, but still continue to install carpet part time. I didn't have a book like this to learn from, I learned on the job, but a book like this would have helped me tremendously. I would like to think that for all of the years I've put into this business that this book will make a long term difference. So I am writing this book to help others along the way to fulfill their dreams.

Good Luck!

PREFACE
WHO SHOULD READ THIS BOOK

EMPLOYEE TRAINING / INSTALLERS ASSISTANTS

If you're just starting to work for someone as an employee or assistant, and are new to the Floor covering business you will need a good knowledge of the basic procedures and terms before setting foot on the job. It is very difficult for someone to train you on the job and have the work completed in a timely and professional manner, all at the same time. No one wants a complete beginner installing new carpet in their home.

TO THOSE PREPARING TO START THEIR OWN CARPET INSTALLATION BUSINESS

This book will teach you all of the fundamentals of Installation so that you can find work with a knowledgeable Installer and develop the hands on training necessary to start your own Floor covering business in the least amount of time.
    One of the most Important aspects for success in the carpet business is the quality of your work. You need a thorough knowledge and experience level. You must work with a professional installer for at least two years to get the hands on experience necessary for your reputation and skill level to maximize.
    It is also necessary to have a minimum of two years of experience to become level one certified with the International Certified Floorcovering Installers Association (CFI.)

DO IT YOURSELF INSTALLATION

The do it yourself installer can follow the step by step procedures of Installation and install their own carpet in their own home. I would recommend starting with small rooms and first using an inexpensive carpet to practice with before trying anything larger.

SECTION I
THE BASICS

Art Work: © 2002 Eric M. Larson

ON THE JOB EXPERIENCE

If I were to tell you that reading this book would instantly turn you into a expert installer I would be lying. A professional musician can't learn the skills to play an instrument by reading a book and its the same with carpet installation.

Many of the skills require some practice in learning the correct techniques. Although, studying the material in this book will speed your learning the skills and techniques tremendously. The combination of studying the material in this handbook and working on the job with a skilled professional carpet installer is the intended method of study. Using this method you will reach the advanced level quickly. Review the handbook before and after work.

Studying this Handbook for a week in advance of starting on the job will insure that your first day runs as smoothly as possible and will give you a good basic understanding of what you are to do.

An excellent way to practice the skills of installation is to install carpet in your own home. The best way to learn new skills is by doing them. Try stretching in carpet in one area of your home and gluing down carpet in another area of your home.

There is a tremendous amount of work to be done on the job so it is difficult for your boss to explain everything on the job. Don't be afraid to ask questions but save most of your difficult questions for before and after work. Focus on what you are doing and you will be amazed at how quickly you learn.

The combination of reviewing the handbook and training on the job will have you working up to speed quickly with a minimal amount of mistakes.

PROPER LANGUAGE, APPEARANCE AND CLEANLINESS

No matter how good your work looks if you leave a bad impression with the customer then it was not a job well done. Dressing in a clean professional manner will reflect that your work is also top notch. Imagine if you were having carpet installed in your home and a couple of renegades showed up dressed in rags. You would have serious concerns as to whether their work will look as bad as they do.

The work you are doing is physical labor so the clothing you wear may reflect that, but that is no reason to look like a slob. Wear clothing loose enough so that you can get up and down throughout the day. Wear clean clothing, use good language and keep yourself clean in other people's homes. When your clothing begins to look old and tattered purchase new clothing. Installing carpet is not a dirty job, so you do not need to dress like a roofer, in fact dirty clothing will only get the new carpet dirty.

HAIR LENGTH

Many companies argue that men must have short hair for appearance, but what hair length makes your appearance look better? This is purely a matter of personal preference. While every one agrees that being dirty and not bathing is offensive, this has nothing to do with hair length.

Women have the right to have long hair, while men on the same job often do not. Your hair length has nothing to do with your sexual gender. Hair length regulations are a sex specific type of discrimination.

Your hair length does not affect your work performance on most jobs. But if your job has inherent danger, or your work is affected by very long hair then it is justified to have a regulation for anyone with long hair to keep it pulled back. This is the case with installing carpet; there is a danger in running power tool and it is very difficult to see what you are doing with long hair over your face. I suggest that you keep it pulled back for your own safety.

I fully support mens right to have long hair. Society has created false stereo types for men with long hair, *you have the right to have long hair*, and any employer or customer that judges you badly for having long hair is discriminating against your human rights.

TATTOOS

Society has also stereo typed tattooed people, you still have the right to have tattoos. Whether you like tattoos or not is a matter of personal preference. Your employer does not have the right to tell you that you can not have or show tattoos.

You were probably expecting me to tell you that you should keep your tattoos covered when working but I think this is an important human rights issue and I am not going to support an unfair work regulation. Tattoos are a human right, you have the right to have and show tattoos.

Discrimination is somewhat different than a human right. With discrimination, you are being discriminated against for something out of your control, such as skin color. But with human rights **this is something you want to do** - IT IS YOUR RIGHT. A person who doesn't like you because you have tattoos, is also discriminating against you because they are judging you with an unreal stereotype about tattoos.

If you are working in other peoples homes, they may discriminate against you for having tattoos, but this is their problem not yours. The person discriminating against you and your human right to have tattoos is in the wrong.

CLOTHING THAT I RECOMMEND FOR INSTALLING CARPET

1.   JEANS I prefer wearing long pants over shorts. It protects your knees and is more comfortable when wearing kneepads. You will be on your hands and knees a lot and you need all the protection you can get. Some installers do prefer to wear shorts in hot weather, but then wear kneepads also. If you like wearing shorts that's OK but always wear knee pads whether you wear jeans or shorts. Kneepads not only protect your skin from abrasion, but also from the continuous pressure that can cause fluid buildup on your knees (known as roofers knee).

Several brands of pants are available with kneepads built into the knees, you may prefer wearing these types of pants rather than wearing kneepads.

The pants should be loose enough so that you are comfortable getting up and down all day. If you have trouble keeping your pants up wear a belt. Wear pants that are rugged enough to hold up to a lot of stress and abuse.

2.   TEE SHIRTS You will get warm when your are working, and you will want to wear a light weight cotton tee shirt. If it's cold out you may want to wear layers of clothing and strip off the layers as you get warmed up. If the weather is cold outside wear a coat that is tough enough to hold up to some abuse. The backing of the carpet is very abrasive so you will want to wear clothing that can hold up to that. Carrying in carpet is hard on your clothes and skin because the backing is very coarse and you may want to wear a long sleeved shirt to protect your arms from abrasion as well.

3.   BOOTS OR SNEAKERS Purchase shoes that will hold up to being on your hands and knees a lot, as this tends to wear them out quickly. You also want shoes that are comfortable to wear all day. The toes of your shoes are always the first to go. Some carpet installers buy steel toed shoes or boots. This allows the shoes longer wear but the leather still wears out on the toe more quickly than the rest of the shoe. I purchase multiple pairs of work shoes and rotate their wear with other activities to balance out the wear pattern so that their life is extended. I've noticed that some black soled shoes can leave scuff marks on light colored carpet, its not very common but none the less a thought to consider.

SHOE SOLES

A smooth soled shoe is less likely to track in dirt and mud, yet if you're working in slick snow carrying in a heavy roll of carpet can become very dangerous if you slip. A chunky soled shoe will track in more dirt and mud, and when you're Installing carpet that is not good, but once everythings carried in you're not going to have the tracking in problem.

You have to consider the weather conditions and the conditions at the particular house where you will be working. If you know that there is going to be slick snow or icy sidewalks and hills to walk up you must save your neck and wear a shoe with good traction.

You can keep a spare pair of shoes with you so you'll have a clean pair once everything's inside.

4.   GLOVES You will be carrying in a lot of tools from outside and you may want to wear gloves during cold wintery conditions. Purchase some gloves that are flexible enough so that you can use your fingers. I prefer to wear leather gloves without any lining so that I have better use of my hands. Thickly lined gloves may be warmer but when you're working with your hands it becomes a detriment.

Just remember that your clothes should be clean as well as yourself. You will be working in others peoples homes and you want to project a good image. In a customer's home you should be polite and courteous at all times. Never curse or use foul language.

QUIZ - The Basics
Section 1 - Part 1

1. The proper clothing for work should be?
   (a) Clean and comfortable.
   (b) Not too clean because you'll be getting dirty anyway.
   (c) Anything you can find that is clean.
   (d) Long sleeved shirts and no shoes.

2. When working in someones home?
   (a) You can say anything you want because it is none of their business.
   (b) Be polite and courteous.
   (c) You will get mad and curse a lot.
   (d) Both A and C.

3. You can leave a bad impression with the customer even if you did a good job by...
   (a) using inappropriate language.
   (b) not being clean.
   (c) wearing old tattered clothing.
   (d) all of the above.

4. You become skilled as a carpet installer by...
   (a) simply studying this book.
   (b) by believing that you are a great installer.
   (c) by studying this book, believing in yourself, and working on the job with a skilled carpet installer.
   (d) none of the above.

5. Purchase shoes that ...
   (a) have black soles.
   (b) are high tops.
   (c) hold up to being on your hands and knees, as the toes tend to wear out quickly.
   (d) smooth soled.

Answers
   1. A   2. B   3. D   4. C   5. C

DEFINITIONS AND TERMS

ACTION BACK - General term for a type of carpet backing made of a synthetic fiber. Most carpet backings are action back today. Has a mesh backing that is coated with latex. The quality is rated by the size of the grids in the meshing, a 12 pic backing has smaller grids than a 5 pic. Normally looks white in color. Requires being stretched with a power stretcher to lay smooth for its life. Can be glued directly to the floor or double glued over a cushion. Seaming is done with a hot melt seam tape and iron, or directly glued for a glue down installation.

ADHESIVE - A type of glue that dries to hold materials to a surface. A latex based glue is used to glue carpet direct indoors. A solvent based adhesive is used for an outdoor Installation. A release adhesive can be used for a double glue installation between the pad and the floor. Glue down seam seals are also used by Installers. Adhesive is applied using a trowel, a spray adhesive tank, or a stand up trowel.

ALUMINUM NAILS - They are used to attach concrete tack strip and metals to a concrete floor. A hammer drill is used to drill a small hole, then the aluminum nail is hammered in. Comes in 7/8th and 5/8th of an inch sizes.

AXMINSTER CARPET - A type of carpet that is woven on an axminster loom. It was invented in the U.S.A. in 1878 the height of the Victorian era, giving this carpet historical value. Most axminsters are imported from England, and are named after a town in England. Axminsters bend little in the width, and thus do not stretch much in the width.

BERBER - Type of carpet with loops that can often have a pattern to match on seams. Has a low pile (nap) unlike plush carpet. Berber tends to hold up well to high traffic wear.

BIRD CAGE STEP - Bottom step in which the railing banister and spindles makes a circle that looks like a "bird cage". Bird cage steps must be hand sewn to install in a water fall fashion step.

BORDER - A custom carpet installation in which a different type or color of carpet borders the center piece of carpet, known as the field carpet. The border is the outer carpet that surrounds the field carpet. The pile direction of the border lays towards the field.

BULL NOSED - Method of installing a step so that it is upholstered. Attaching the carpet under the lip of the foot of the step. The carpet runs straight up the riser and wraps around the lip. On most steps the foot of the step (the part that you step on) sticks out farther than the riser. The carpet is attached under this lip and then kicked on to the tack strip. This method is used for a different look opposed to a water fall step. A pie shaped step can be bull nosed. (See section 4 on steps)

CARPET CUSHION - Used under carpet for a soft cushion. Commonly known as carpet pad. Also less commonly called carpet underlay. Is manufactured in various types such as rebond pad, foam pad, and double glue pad. Comes in various densities commonly 6 lb. or 8 lb. pads. The higher pound pads being firmer. Pads of various thicknesses are used: 7/16 inch for

Pictured is a utility knife for cutting carpet and pad. I prefer a carpet knife that used slotted blades rather than a utility knife.

Pictured is a gillie gun, also known as an electric stapler. It uses narrow staples that will hide better in carpet. The stapler is used for rolled edges, upholstery work and in some tight areas like closets. Excessive stapling is not recommended, it can show dimples in the carpet. The glue gun is preferred.

residential and 3/8th for commercial installations.

CARPET KNIFE - A utility knife, or a knife with slotted blades, (slotted blades are sharp on both sides.) Used to cut carpet. A utility knife has a blade that is sharp on only one side.

CONCRETE STRIP - Correctly known as concrete tackless strip. Concrete strip is a slang term used on jobs instead of saying tackless. It is tack strip with concrete nails pre set into the wood strips. Shorter and wider masonry nails are used in nailing the tack strip to a concrete floor. All tackless strip is made of wood with steel pins set in them to grip the carpet when stretching, but concrete strip has masonry nails pre set into them to nail to the floor.

CUSTOM CARPET - Carpet that is custom made by an installer using rug making techniques, such as borders, inlays, and carpet carving. Can be installed in a home or made into an area rug.

CUT PILE - The surface yarns that make up the pile (nap) of the carpet are cut. Not a level loop or berber. This is the style of carpet in a plush carpet.

DENIER - The weight of the surface yarn. The higher the number the larger the surface yarn. A higher denier will attribute to a higher density pile.

DENSITY - The pile density is determined by the closeness of the surface yarns (pitch or gauge) and the thickness of the surface yarns (denier). Heavy plush carpets have a higher density pile.

DOUBLE GLUE INSTALLATION - A type of installation in which the pad is glued directly to the floor and the carpet is glued directly to the pad. A specific type of pad must be used for this type of installation. This installation is excellent for areas that are to large to power stretch, but require a padding. Correct trowel notch size and adhesive types are essential for this type of installation. Between pad and floor a trowel notch that covers 20 yards per gallon of adhesive is used. Between pad and carpet a trowel that cover 5 yards per gallon of adhesive is used.

DROP ROOM - The room is carpeted without any seams. (The room drops without any seams.) Most carpets are 12 feet wide so the room would be less than 12 feet wide. Carpet can come in widths up to 15 feet wide.

DUCT TAPE - Used to tape pad seams together especially on concrete floors. Used to patch tears in the pad. Used to tape the pad on steps where it wraps over the lip, this protects the pad. Also used to tape cords and cables to the wall, out of the way.

Pictured is the knee kicker.

Pictured is my main tool box, it contains a knee kicker, trimmer, spreader, duck tape, pad stapler, rubber mallet, hammer, nail bar, scrapper, acoustical nails, row cutter, common nails, tack strip nails, pad staples, and masonry nails.

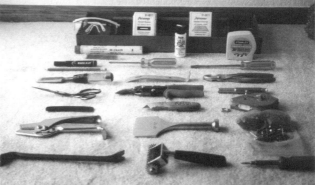

The tray contains a pry bar, seam tractor, screw drivers, tack strip cutters, stair tool, gold nails, comb (for seams), utility knife, chalk line, scissors, aviation snips, nail punch, chisel, base remover, pliers, screw drivers, marker and pencil, scraper blades, carpet cleaner, tape measure, safety glasses, trimmer & knife blades.

ELECTRA SEAM TAPE - Seam tape that uses a low volt current to melt the tape adhesive, eliminating the need for a hot melt iron. Twenty four feet of seaming can be completed in approximately 4 minutes.

FIELD CARPET - The center carpet that is surrounded by a border carpet.

FOAM PAD - A softer pad that does not last as long as a rebond pad. Made of a foam urethane. Tends to have a lower poundage than a rebond pad, giving it a softer feel, shorter life, and a lower density.

GILLIE GUN - Electric stapler that is used in a variety of places. Is used on upholstered steps

Pictured is the nail bar. Used to nail under ledges that can not be nailed with a hammer.

and in tight places that can not be stretched, like the side walls in a very small closet or around a toilet, but a glue gun is preferred for these applications, because staples will show dimples in many low piled plush carpets.

GLUE GUN - Electric or gas glue gun that holds glue sticks (thermal adhesive) and is used for the ends of seam, carpet patching and steps. Used for upholstery work on steps, capped ends etc. It is used to hold the carpet to the tack strip in tight areas, like around toilets. A glue gun is used for seam welding, gluing the backing directly together on seams. Can also be used as a thermal seam seal instead of latex. This is applied to the cut edge for seams, then seamed causing it to melt and bond the cut edges. This is similar to seam welding.

HACKER - Slang term for a carpet installer that does a very poor job.

HAND SEWING - Joining carpet by sewing with a needle and thread. Prior to the invention of hot melt seam tape, and the seam iron all carpet seams were hand sewn. Today hand sewing is used only for speciality situations, because the hand sewn seam does not open up as much when bent. Used for seaming woven carpet backings that are not back sized to hold a hot melt seam tape. Used for any situations in which the carpet is to be bent over a surface; this includes a bird cage step installed in the water-fall fashion and wrapping carpet over any ledge.

HOT MELT SEAM TAPE - A meshed seam tape that is coated with a thermal adhesive. Used to seam carpet seams together. Adhesive is melted with a seam iron. Is used with a carpet backing that is suitable for hot melt seaming.

INSURED - Insurance carried by the installer, to protect against liability. Protects the installer in case of customer injury or home damages.

JUTE BACK - The backing looks like a burlap sack. It is brown, if it has not been bleached. Made of a natural fiber that comes from the inner bark of the Corchorus tree. A woody shrub in the linden family, that is found in Asia. Very few carpets have this type of backing today. Can be stretched and installed over pad or can be glued directly to the floor. Seaming is done with hot melt seam tape, or directly glued for a glue down installation.

KANGA BACK - This carpet has the foam pad (cushion) attached to the back. Also called foam back. Does not require to be stretched. Can be stapled, taped, or glued direct. An enhancer backed carpet also has an attached cushion.

KNEE KICKER - Used to set carpet on tack strip and move the carpet into place. Has teeth

that grip the carpet on one end and a foam pad on the other side to kick with your knee.

LATEX - Many adhesives are latex based. Seam seal is made of latex, it is used to seal the cut edge on areas to be seamed. Carpet backing's are often covered in latex from the factory and they appear white in color.

LEVEL LOOP - Carpet that has a low nap (pile) and has loops somewhat like Berber. Tends to be slightly lighter weight and less expensive than Berber, yet is also known to hold up well to traffic.

LOOPED PILE - The surface yarns that make up the pile (nap) are looped. This is the pile style of a berber carpet and level loop carpet, but a plush has a cut pile.

MAIN TOOL BOX - This is the tool box that contains most of the vital tools that are needed on *every* job. It is carried in for almost ever job.

MASONARY NAIL - A steel nail used for nailing into concrete. Come in various sizes and

Pictured is a hallway full of scraps after an installation.

Pictured is a row cutter for cutting the edge of the carpet off for seams. Not to be mistaken for a row runner.

Pictured is the seam box and all of its contents, seam tape, seam iron, extension cord, glue gun & glue sticks, latex, and the seam mate which is not kept in the seam box.

Pictured is the power stretcher. A power stretcher is used to stretch the carpet.

lengths. Used for nailing concrete tackstrip. Long masonry nails can be used for difficult concrete situations such as cracks in the floor near metal positions. Masonry nails can be used instead of aluminum nails.

MASONARY BIT - Drill bit that is used for drilling into concrete. Carpet installers use these to attach tack strip and metals.

METAL - A general term used for the metals that finish off the carpet edges next to vinyl floors, usually in kitchen and bathrooms. A pin metal is used for stretch in carpet and a pinless type is used for a glue down installation. A stair nose metal is used on the top of a step with a vinyl landing. A flat bar metal is used in certain situations in which the height of the floor transitions are different. Flat bars are used in some situations on both stretch in and glue down installations.

MISS MATCHED PATTERN - A seam in a patterned carpet that is seamed together and the pattern was not perfectly matched, causing the seam to show.

NAIL BAR - Used to nail in difficult to reach places like under toe kicks.

NAP - The top fibers of the carpet that you walk

on are the nap. Nap is technically called the pile. Nap is the individual surface yarns or looped yarns depending on the type of carpet. (See berber, level loop and plush carpets below). The nap thickness is determined by the density of the nap. Carpet has a nap (pile) direction that must run the same direction when laying different pieces of carpet together or the carpet will look a different color in different rooms or in seams.

OPEN TIME - The amount of time between spreading an adhesive on the floor and laying the carpet into the glue. Adhesive should become tacky before laying the carpet into the adhesive. When finger testing, strings should be present.

PAD - The cushion under a stretch in carpet. Pad is the common term, while carpet cushion is the technical term. Comes in various thicknesses from 1/4 inch to 1/2 inch. Comes in various poundages (density) commonly of 6 lb. to 8 lb.

Pictured is a seam mate, they come in different widths for different doorway widths.

Pictured is the spreader. It's used with the power stretcher when stretching to hold the carpet into the corner and hold it on to the tack strip.

And is available in various types of rebond or foam urethane pads. See rebond pad.

PATTERN MATCH - Carpet that has a pattern that needs to be matched at the seams. Berber tends to have a pattern match most often.

PILE - The technical industry term for carpet nap. The surface yarns that make up the top of the pile. The pile has a direction that it lays, and all seam areas must run the same direction, in attached pieces of carpet.

PLUSH - Carpet that has a cut pile of surface yarns. The surface yarns are longer than they are with a berber, commercial carpet, or level loop. The Pile (nap) stands in individual strands, while the surface yarns in berbers and level loop carpets are looped.

POWER STRETCHER - Used to stretch carpet. Always use a power stretcher to install carpet over pad. The head of the stretcher has teeth that grip the carpet when stretching and a handle to push down on using leverage to stretch the carpet. Multiple tubes can be attached to extend across the room. The foot of the stretcher pushes against the opposite wall as you push down on the handle to stretch the carpet.

QUARTER ROUND - Half round wood strips nailed around the perimeter of the lower floor, generally used to cover the edge for vinyl and hardwood floors. Carpet can be installed but it is not recommended to install carpet with quarter round on.

REBOND PAD - A heavier density pad (cushion) than a foam pad. It is made from pieces of recycled pad. Looks like multi colored specks of pad.

RESTRETCH - A carpet that has been stretched before, but has wrinkled and needs to be stretched again.

RISER - The upright part of the step that is not walked on (between the foot or tread of the step that you step on).

ROW CUTTER - Used to cut carpet for seams. All carpets have rows including plush, traditionally only Berber and level loop carpets were row cut on seams. In the past plush carpets were always cut using a straight edge. This tool cuts between the rows for seams.

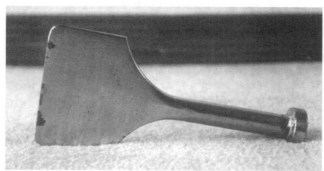

Pictured is a stair tool used to place the carpet into the corner of the steps so that it stays tight on the step. It also creates a crease for a pleasing look.

Pictured to the is a Seam tractor. These come in different types such as steel (star tracktor) as shown or plastic.

ROW RUNNER - A tool that is used before row cutting to spread open the rows in the nap and create a line to follow when row cutting. A comb or straight screwdriver can be used as a row runner, there are also row separators that can be purchased specifically for this purpose. This tool does not cut the carpet the **row cutter** does.

SALVAGE EDGE - The edge of the carpet as it comes from the factory. This edge is cut off in seam areas with a row cutter or straight edge so the seam fits together without any overlapping or gaps. You want a good edge without any loss of pile for an effective seam (one that is not easily seen.)

SCULPTURED - Carpet with different heights of carpet nap (pile) that creates a pattern or design. May be a solid color or multi colored carpet but the sculptured look is made by differing height in the nap.

SCRAPS - Pieces of carpet and pad that are left after trimming the carpet and pad. These will be recycled or thrown away. Larger pieces that are left from cut outs in a room are left for the customer.

SEAM BOX - Tool box designed for a seamer. Holds seamer, seam tape, glue gun and extension cord.

SEAM IRON - Tool that heats up to melt the seam tape. Its placed on top of the seam tape under the carpet seam and moved along as the glue melts, and the carpet is seamed together.

A vinyl knife is often used as a tucker, for tucking the carpet.

Pictured is a wall trimmer for trimming stretch in carpet. It trims the carpet to just the right length to tuck next to the wall.

SEAM TAPE - Tape with glue on the top for seaming together carpet. A seam Iron is used to melt the glue that is placed under the carpet seam. Known as hot-melt tape.

SEAM SEALING - Using latex in an adhesive bottle to seal the cut edge of carpet for seams. Seam sealing prevents the carpet from fraying or raveling in the seams. If there is a problem with the installation, a black light will be used to test for the use of seam seal by the carpet mill. On glue down carpet installations a contact cement type of adhesive is used for seam sealing.

SEAM MATE - A tool used to cut seams in doorways.

SOFT BACK CARPET - Type of carpet backing that has a soft cloth over the backing so that it won't scratch woodwork. Installs the same as action back carpets.

SPREADER - Is used to press and hold the carpet on to the tack strip when power stretching.

SQUARE - Used to square carpet on cross seams and the starting ends of steps to make a square 90% cut.

STAIR TOOL - Resembles a large chisel without a sharp edge, used to force the carpet between the tack strip to hold the carpet on steps securely and create a crease in the stair corner.

STRAIGHT EDGE - Used to cut carpet for seams and steps.

STRETCH - IN - Carpet installed over pad with tack strip around the perimeter of the room. Jute back, action back, wilton and axminster carpets can be stretched in to a room over a separate pad. Not all carpets can be stretched over pad, some are only for direct glue installations.

SURFACE YARN - The surface fiber (yarn) that makes up the top of the carpet that you walk on.

TACK STRIP - Wood strips with sharp pins attached for stretching carpet. Tack strip is nailed around the perimeter of the room to stretch carpet. Short for tackless strip, (see below).

TACKLESS STRIP - Wood strips with sharp pins attached for stretching carpet. Tackless strip is nailed around the perimeter of the room to stretch carpet. Comes prenailed with wood or concrete nails. Comes in various widths of 3/4 inch up to 2 inch commercial wide. Slang terms are "wood strip" and "concrete strip, and tack strip." Tri tack has three rows of pins rather than two and is 1 1/4 inch wide, this is the preferred type of tack strip.

TEETH - Metal pins in knee kicker and power stretcher that grip the carpet.

TOOL POUCH - Holds your knife tucker and other tools if you like.

TOE KICKS - The riser under counters in kitchens and bathrooms. Sometimes they are carpeted. Tack strip is nailed under these with a nail bar.

THRESHOLD - A raised surface under a door, that keeps the air sealed out of the home.

TRACTOR - A tool used to press the carpet into hot glue when seaming. Known as a seam tractor. A plastic type is used instead of a steel type(star tractor) on plush carpets because it does not leave marks in the carpet. The marks are most often not permanent but can permanently damage the nap fibers from the points of the steel roller pressing the nap down. A steel tractor gives a good bond with the carpet backing and adhesive. You will not have the problem of the nap being pressed down with a berber carpet.
The steel star tractor is used as a means to break down the seam tape, (only in cool seams) that are peaking (peaking is a raised, peaked area down the seam line that causes the seam to show. Most often in cross lighted areas.) Star tractors are also used for direct glue carpet seams.

TRIMMER - A tool used for trimming carpet to the wall after its been stretched and set on the tack strip.

TRIMMING - Cutting the carpet along the wall using a wall trimmer after the carpet has been stretched or glued direct.

TRIMMER BLADES - Razor blades that are replaceable and used in the wall trimmer.

TROWEL - Used to spread adhesive onto the floor when gluing carpet down direct. Also used for gluing pad in a double glue carpet installation, and for attaching various tiles, and vinyl flooring. Trowels come in various sized notches that spread a specific amount of adhesive per gallon. Trowels come in a U notch, square notch and V notch; a U notch and V notch leaves a larger amount of adhesive than the square. Select the proper trowel notch for the type of installation and product you are installing.

Consider the coarseness of the floor you are applying to, a rougher floor leaves more adhesive on the floor and you can use a smaller notch trowel. Consider the type of carpet that you are gluing. Trowels are also used to install vinyl flooring and mortar for ceramic tile. Use the correct size of trowel for the material you are gluing.

TUCKER - A tool used to tuck carpet along walls after stretching and trimming. Many people use a vinyl knife as a carpet tucker including myself; just dull the sharp edges. Plastic safety tuckers are preferred by many, they prevent scratching of wood work.

TUCKING - You tuck carpet after its been trimmed. You use a tucker tool to push the carpet between the tack strip and the wall to make the carpet look smooth along the edges. The carpet is tucked into the gully - the space between the wall and the tack strip, this space is usually the thickness of your fingers or 3/8th of an Inch.

TUBES - Used in the power stretcher. The tubes are adjustable and extend up to 5 feet each. Multiple tubes are attached to extend across the full length of the room.

TUFTED CARPET - A carpet manufacturing method in which the pile yarns are inserted in to the primary backing. The carpet is manufactured using the tufting process. A tufted carpet is not woven.

UNITARY BACKING - Type of carpet backing that is coated with a high quality latex. Most do not have a meshing (action backing) on the back but some unitary carpets are action backed. This makes it difficult to determine that it is a unitary backed carpet. Some are smooth and some are rough. Used only for direct glue applications.

UPHOLSTERED STEP - Steps that have capped ends, bull nosed, or a pie step. A step that has capped ends does not have a wall along one or both sides, instead the ends are capped. A bird cage step is round and has a circular hand rail that the spindles form what looks like a bird cage. (See section 4 on steps)

VELVET CARPET - A Carpet woven on a velvet loom, either a cut pile or a loop pile. Normally in a solid color but may have a pattern.

WATERFALL - The carpet flows down the riser, not forming to the riser wrapping around the lip. Steps have straight walls along both sides, or capped ends. Contrasting to a bull nosed step: Water fall steps are not **bullnosed.** Carpet flows down over the steps like a waterfall. (See section 4 on steps)

WILTON CARPET - A type of carpet weave. A woven carpet. Probably started the weaving loom industry, with the carpet factory in Wilton, England in 1655. Wilton carpets are of high quality as well as historical value.

WOOD STRIP - Used to stretch the carpet on to its sharp pins, to hold the stretch of carpet. Short for Tackless strip with pre set wood nails. Wood strip has longer nails for nailing to the wood floors. Also known as wood tack strip, tack strip is short for the word tackless strip.

WOVEN GOODS - Carpet that is manufactured on carpet looms such as Axminster carpets, Wiltons, and Velvets. Axminster and velvet looms allow up to 26 different colors and pile heights. The surface yarns are woven across sturdy weft shots that run across the width of the carpet and next to the chain warp shots. Most area rugs are of this type of construction. A high end type of carpet, often with historical value. Many Woven carpets backings must be seamed by hand sewing rather than seamed with hot melt seam tape. Woven carpets can be stretched in or glued direct. Axminster backings stretch more in the length than in the width and most often, wilton and velvets stretch more in the width.

Z -BAR - A type of metal that is used to finish off edges in door ways. Creates a look like the carpet is rolled with out a metal. Tack strip is placed next to the z-bar to hold the stretch. This avoids the use of staples but causes a hard feeling when walking on it. Some times the tack strip pins can be felt through the carpet.

DUTIES OF THE INSTALLERS ASSISTANT

It is not of importance where we stand, but in what direction we are moving.

The duties as an assistant change as your level of experience increases. I've divided the duties of installation into beginner and advanced. This list can be used as a quick start up list as you further study SECTION II: THE PROCE-DURES OF INSTALLATION.

The beginners duties are not technical and anyone can do these from the very start. The advanced duties are more technical and require some practice. At first observe the more ad-vanced tasks being performed, before jumping in and giving it a try yourself. Watching is a big part of learning, it's just as important as practic-ing the skill, but don't just stand around or stand in the way!

Study each of these procedures and write down this list to carry with you until you have it memorized. Further study each procedure in section II.

Every installer has a slightly different system and you should go over this list and ask the person you're working with what he expects from you. Develop a routine with the person you are working with so that you both know exactly what you are to be doing. There is never any reason to be standing around. There is always something to do. For instance, one person can take off the doors while the other is installing tack strip, once the doors are removed and placed out of the way, start Installing the metals or carrying in the pad.

The first step in any job is determining the tools and supplies needed for it. It's a waste of time to carry in the seam box if there are no seams to be done or if you are gluing down a carpet direct you obviously won't need the power stretcher. The same goes for the tack strip, if all of the tack strip has been installed previ-ously and is in good shape don't bring it in.

Don't waste your time carrying in tools and supplies you don't need. If you are working on a wood floor you will not need the Hammer drill to attach the tack strip and metals. The person you are working for will know what is needed for the job so ask.

These steps are for stretch in carpet and if you are gluing carpet direct they will obviously be different. You will not need as many tools for a glue down job. For a direct glue down job you will not need pad or tack strip, or the power stretcher. You will need adhesive and a trowel, you will also need a roller to press the carpet into the glue.

DIVIDING TASKS

It's so important to develop a routine with the person you are working with, once you do your work will become much quicker and effi-cient. Divide up these tasks in an efficient manner so that you are always working. For example:

First person is removing doors and install-ing metals - *Second person* is installing tack strip.

First person is stapling the pad - *Second person* is trimming the pad.

First person is stretching the carpet - *Second person* is setting, trimming and tucking it, and so on through out the list.

At first, just observe and watch the more advanced duties and ask some questions if you don't feel comfortable trying them at first. Eventually you'll learn to do everything. Most installers prefer that a beginner just watch the seaming, stretching and trimming at first. Re-member that there is *always something that you can be doing*. There is **never** a reason to stand around.

Don't be afraid to ask questions if you don't understand something but save your more com-plicated questions for before and after the job. There is so much work to be done on the job that you do not want to be distracting by asking too many questions during the job.

Remember to write down this list and carry

LIST BEGINNERS DUTIES

1. Carry in all tools and supplies needed for the job.

2. Removing old carpet and pad, if the customer hasn't done so.

3. Remove doors that open into the area to be carpeted and mark so they can be returned to their correct location.

4. Install the tack strip if it will be needed. (Not needed for glue down)

5. Installing metals

6. Sweeping the floor.

7. Carry in the padding.

8. Load the hammer stapler with staples. (on a concrete floor you will use a pad glue instead of the stapler)

9. Stapling padding. (or gluing on concrete)

10. Tapeing or stapling pad seams.

11. Trimming padding.

12. Help carry in the carpet rolls.

13. Help lay out the carpet.

14. Picking up carpet and pad scraps.

15. Replacing trimmer blades.

16. Getting the power stretcher and setting it up prior to stretching.

17. Getting the seamer set up and plugged in prior to starting the seams.

18. Tucking the carpet after it has been trimmed.

19. Loading all tools and supplies back into the van in their proper location.

20. Loading all scraps and any old carpet that is to be hauled away.

21. Throwing all garbage into dumpster.

22. Sweeping out the van.

23. If there are steps, tack strip and pad the steps.

MORE ADVANCED DUTIES OF THE ASSISTANT

1. Stretching of the carpet.

2. Setting carpet on the tack strip with knee kicker.

3. Kicking in closets.

4. Trimming carpet.

5. Helping prepare seams by, latexing, row cutting or straight edging.

6. Some seaming of carpet.

7. Installing step carpet, kicking on step carpet.

it with you until you have it memorized and go over this list with your partner so that you are working with one another and not against each other.

TOOLS YOU MAY WANT TO PURCHASE

As an assistant you may want to or be required to put together your own tool box. I will list the most basic tools for you to start with. You will also want to purchase or borrow from someone a scribe to mark your name on your tools.

Discuss with the person you are working with whether or not it would be beneficial for you to purchase your own tool box and some of your own tools. It's more comfortable to at least have your own tool belt and pouch. Owning your own knife and knee pads also is much more comfortable than using someone else's.

These tools can be purchased at a minimal cost. You may not need all of these tools right away but can purchase them over time. The knee kicker and trimmer are more expensive tools and you may want to purchase them as your finances allow.

Basic Tools You May Want to Purchase

The cost of your tools will vary depending on your choice of brands and quality.

1. **Carpet knife** $ 8-12

2. **Carpet tucker** $ 8-12

3. **Tool belt** $ 15-20

4. **Tool pouch** $ 10-15

Below are all of the tools in my main tool box; this tool box is used on every job. In the following section I will list all of these tool along with all of the tools used for carpet installation.

5. **Knee pads** $ 25-30

6. **Tool Box** $ 25-50

7. **Hammer** $ 15-20

8. **Aviation snips** - for cutting metals, and they can be used for cutting tact strip $ 15-20

9. **Straight screw driver** $ 5-10

10. **Phillips screw driver** $ 5-10

Total **costs $131-$199**

SOME MISCELLANEOUS ITEMS YOU MAY NEED

**Small lunch cooler
water jug**

CONTRACTOR OR EMPLOYEE

Often times a carpet store or another carpet installer will hire you but does not consider you to be an employee. This is called subcontracting. If you are working for someone that subcontracts work from you then you are in reality a self employed contractor and need to keep an income and expenditure log. The person you are working for subcontracts work from you and gives you a 1099 form at the end of the year. They do not pay your taxes for you. Many times an assistant or apprentice is consider to be a self employed contractor.

If you are an employee then you will be told how much you will be paid, when and at what time you will work, and what to wear. Your company will pay your tax payments, social security, and workmen comp. Your boss will give you a W-2 Form at the end of the year that shows your income for the year.

If you are self employed you will tell them what you charge, when you will work, and you will give them a bill for the work you did. You will also make your own quarterly tax payments if you are a self employed contractor.

You will need a Federal ID # to put on your tax forms. You acquire a federal ID # by contacting the Internal revenue service. Look under the federal government section in the phone book for the number.

You are a business and will need a business name for example Toms Floor Covering. The person you are working for will show you on their tax forms. You are responsible to pay your own taxes.

A business pays quarterly estimates on taxes four times a year using form 1040 ES. Just estimate how much you think you will make for the year, and send in your quarterly payments on the due dates for federal and state taxes. Estimation sheets are available with tax workbooks from the IRS. Keep a record sheet of how much money you pay in for federal and state taxes, you will need to know how much you paid when you file your taxes. If you paid in enough then you may receive money back, or if you did not pay

enough you will owe money at the time of filing.

You will need to keep track of all of your expenses and income. This can be done with business management software, or an income and expenditure ledger from an office supply store. Write down everything you are paid in your income ledger, or input on an invoice on the computer. Write down all of your expenses in your expenditure ledger or input on the computer.

You can purchase a business ledger at an office supply store or make one using a spread sheet on a computer. Computer software that I recommend for managing your business are Quick Books, MYOB, and Peach Tree.

Keep a file cabinet for all of your purchase receipts such as tools, supplies, and equipment. Work clothing can be used but only uniforms or clothing with your business name on it can be claimed. A vehicle that you use for work only can either be depreciated or you can keep a mileage log. Keep records of all of your vehicle maintenance, you may not be able to use every thing but it is a good idea to keep the records.

At the end of each month review your income and expenses. Total all of your income and expenses if you use a ledger. At the end of the year total every thing up and you will have all of your income and expenses for your taxes. The more expenses you have the less you will pay in taxes.

You should purchase an Individual Retirement Account (IRA) and deposit money in it monthly or all at once each year. This will reduce your taxes and allow you to retire one day. Look into a Sep and IRA at a discount broker (TD Waterhouse) or at your local bank. You will be glad you did when you get older and want to retire.

You may want to hire an accountant to help you with all of this book keeping. Find someone well in advance to help you set up your record keeping system and supply you with the forms you will need. When tax time comes around you will have all of your records straight and have someone to do your taxes.

COMPLETE TOOL CHECK LIST
FOR STRETCH IN CARPET

CARPET STRETCHING TOOLS

Power stretcher

Stretcher Tubes for power stretcher; they attach together to extend across the room.
Each tube will extend to five feet, you need enough to span the longest room. Tubes are extending from the apposing wall.

5 Foot two by four to stretch away from the wall for protection of the wall.

Pictured is an older style powerstretcher.

Knee kicker is used to hook the carpet on to the tackstrip and move the carpet for positioning.

Pictured is a kneekicker.

TRIMMING & CUTTING TOOLS

Carpet Trimmer
The trimmer is pictured on the right. Trimmers are used to trim along the wall after kneekicking and stretching.

Trimmer Blades
Trimmer blades shown to the right. Used in the carpet trimmer.

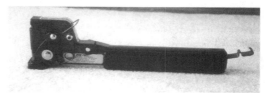

Hammer Stapler for stapling pad.
Hammer stapler pictured.

Staples for the hammer stapler.
Staples pictured right.

Carpet Knife
Photo of a carpet knife with a slotted blade for use on both sides right.

Slotted or utility blades depending on the type of knife. Shown are slotted blades.

(Pictured right) carpet shears. Used to trim nap fibers when seaming.

Photo of a tool belt and pouch, a carpet knife and a tucker.

Knife Blades
Tool Pouch
Tool Belt
Carpet Tucker
Knee Pads

TOOLS FOR SEAMS

Straight Edge (Six foot)
Square
Tape Measure
Row Cutter
Blades for Row Cutter (they may be the same as for your knife)
Comb (for running rows)
Seam Iron
Seam Board (to run behind Iron)
Extension Cord
Hot Melt Seam Tape

Picture is a comb. It can be used to run a row prior to row cutting.

Seam Latex
Glue Gun
Glue Sticks
Seam Tractor
Carpet Shears
Seam Mate (for doorway seams)
Stay Nails (Tack strip nails can be used)

SCREW DRIVERS & HAMMERS & PLIERS

Standard screwdriver
Phillips screwdriver
Claw Hammer
Rubber Mallet

TOOLS FOR STEPS

Stair Tool
Tape Measure
Straight Edge
Square
Stair Nose Metal (If needed)
Gilli Gun

TACK STRIP and SUPPLIES for INSTALLING

Wood Tack Strip
Tack Strip Cutters   Tack strip cutters are used for cutting tack strip. They are not used for cutting any metal.
Tack Strip Nails (2 1/2 Inch nails)
Wood Chisel
A wood chisel is used to cut the occasional piece of tack strip that is already installed.

Picture are tack strip cutters for cutting the tack strip.

METALS and SUPPLIES for INSTALLING METALS

Pin Metals
Tape Measure
Ring Shank Nails to nail pin metals
Aviation Snips   (for cutting metals)
Miter Box
Hack Saw
Flat Bar Metal
Gold Nails - for nailing flat bars and stair nose
bars.

Nail Set

A nail set is used to finished nailing pin metals to avoid hammering down as many of the pins.

photo of nail set

Pictured is the gilli gun in its case.

Pictured are gold nails.Gold nails are used to nail flat bats and stair nose bars.

Pictured ar ring shank nails. They give a good hokd on metals.

MISCELLANEOUS TOOLS

30 Foot Tape Measure
Trash Bags
Sleds for moving appliances
Gilli Gun - electric stapler.
Gilli Gun Staples (9/16th inch)
Heavy Duty **Extension Cord** (15-25 feet long)
Nail Bar (for nailing under toe kicks)

photo of aviation snips

Pry-Bar For removing old tack strip and metals. Also can be used to remove the door pins.

Rubber Mallet - Used to hammer down pin metals. A white head mallet is used so that marks are not left on the metal.

Pictured is a rubber mallet.

Pictured is a pry bar. It's used for prying up tackstrip, metals, and removing the pins in doors.

Chalk
(white) For use in a chalk line.

Chalk Line

Photo of chalk line.

Razor Blade Scraper
Scraper Blades
Plug in Adapter
Broom
Dust Pan
Marking Pen
Plastic Squeeze Bottles (For applying latex & seam seals)
Nail (Sized for removing hinges on doors)
Pencil & note pad
Calculator

Vacuum Cleaner
Carpet Cleaner
Colored Wood Putty
Old English (various colors for rubbing over baseboards after installation to remove scuff marks.)
First Aid Supplies
Cookie Cutter
(for patching burn or stain areas)

Sleds for moving appliances
Scribe (for marking your valuable tools)
Radio - CD - Tape Player

Safety glasses are used to protect your eyes when nailing tack strip into concerete.

ADDITIONAL TOOLS FOR A CONCRETE FLOOR

Hammer Drill (For attaching metals and tack strip on concrete)
Extension Cord & **Adapter**
Carbide Masonry Bits (1/8th inch)
Aluminum Nail (5/8th & 7/8th)
Concrete Tack Strip
(Tack strip with concrete nails pre started)
Concrete Nails
Pad Adhesive
Duck Tape for pad seams
Safety Glasses
Ear Plugs

Optional - **T-Nailer** (used with an air compressor to nail in concrete)

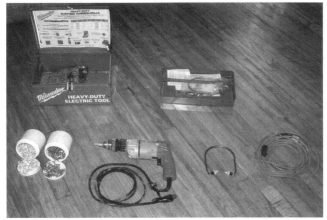

Pictured below is, the hammer drill box, extension cord, hammer drill, ear plugs, 5/8th aluminum nails, 7/8th aluminum nails. The hammer drill is used for attaching tack strip and metals on concrete.

TOOLS FOR DIRECT GLUE DOWN CARPET

Carpet Adhesive (indoor or outdoor) enough to cover the area

Trowel I recommended a 1/8th inch to 3/32 inch V notch Trowel. Trowel size depends on factors such as the type of carpet and the floor surface.

Carpet Roller -100 lb

Glue Down Carpet Trimmer
It is like a trimmer for stretch in carpet only it trims the carpet net to the wall; being that their is no tack strip to tuck it next to. A stretch in carpet trimmer trims the carpet longer.

Seam Seal - For glue down seams. (Solvent based)

Solvent for cleaning glue

Pinless Metals (Have no pins because the carpet is glued directly)

Flat Bar Metal (if needed; pinless metals are preferred)

Pictured is a roller used for glued down carpet installations.

POSITIVE ATTITUDE - SETTING GOALS

People are bout as happy as they make up their minds to be.
  Abe Lincoln

Everything you do begins in your mind. Whether today is a good or bad day is up to you. Your thoughts are the cause of everything. A positive person will turn what some would think was a mistake into a learning experience. You may not notice the amount of negative thoughts that enter your mind throughout the day. Simply by being aware of your thoughts, you will learn to recognize your own thought pattern. Most negative thinking is a result of focusing on unrealistic fears. Once you notice your negative thoughts, you can change them by using positive self-talk. Your thoughts are the way you are talking to yourself. It is important to counter negative thoughts with a positive affirmation. For example, you could say to yourself, I can do it or I am good at this and I keep getting better. Believe in yourself and anything is possible. You cannot control everything that happens to you in life but the one thing you have complete control of is your mind.

You can improve your skills by visualizing yourself doing the act successfully. Visualize yourself possessing the skills and knowledge necessary and you will create a self-fulfilling prophecy. Your dreams become your reality.

Each day set a goal to do a little bit more. Don't be too hard on yourself. You cannot do everything at once. Have confidence in yourself and your abilities, visualize success and set goals. Work hard and think positive and you will be successful.

Our doubts are traitors that make us lose the good we oft might win, by fearing to attempt.
  John Quincy Adams

QUIZ -MULTIPLE CHOICE
SECTION 1 - PART 2

1. What is a trimmer used for?
   (a) Cutting carpet pad next to the tack strip.
   (b) Seaming the carpet together before stretching.
   (c) Cutting the carpet next to the wall after stretching.
   (d) Both a and b.

2. A drop room is one that?
   (a) Drops without any seams.
   (b) Should not be installed.
   (c) Has a lot of seams.
   (d) Is the same as a non drop room.

3. What is a row cutter used for?
   (a) To cut the edge of the carpet between the rows for seams.
   (b) Trimming carpet next to the wall.
   (c) Seaming the carpet together.
   (d) Both a and b.

4. What is a tractor used for?
   (a) Plowing corn fields
   (b) Pressing the carpet into the glue when seaming.
   (c) Seaming the carpet together.
   (d) None of the above.

5. What is the power stretcher.
   (a) Kicking very hard with the knee kicker.
   (b) A new type of carpet.
   (c) A tool that stretches the carpet so that it stays tight.
   (d) Yanking on the carpet really hard.

Answers
1. C 2. A 3. A 4. B 5. C

QUIZ TRUE/FALSE
SECTION 1 - PART 3

T/F 1. You can improve your skills by visuallizing yourself doing the act succesfully.

T/F 2. A Hammer Drill is used for attaching metals and tack strip on wood floors.

T/F 3. **Tack Strip Cutters -** Tack strip cutters are used for cutting carpet and pad.

T/F 4. When subcontracting you are a person that is considered to be self employed.

T/F 5. Save the sales receipts on all your work clothing so that you can possibly use this on your taxes as an expense.

T/F 6. It's so important to develop a routine with the person you are working with, once you do, your work will become much quicker and efficient. For example: First person is removing doors and installing metals - Second person is installing tack strip.

T/F 7. **STAIR TOOL -** Resembles a large chisel without a sharp edge; used to force the carpet between the tack strip to hold the carpet on steps securely and create a crease in the stair corner.

T/F 8. Everything you do begins in your mind. Whether today is a good or bad day is up to you. Your thoughts are the cause of everything.

T/F 9. **QUARTER ROUND -** half round wood strips nailed on the perimeter of the lower floor generally used to cover the edge for vinyl and hardwood floors. Carpet can be installed, but it is not recommended to install carpet with quarter round on.

Answers
1. T   2. F   3. F 4. T   5. T 6. T 7. T
8. T 9. T

First Procedure of Installation
MEASURING FOR CARPET

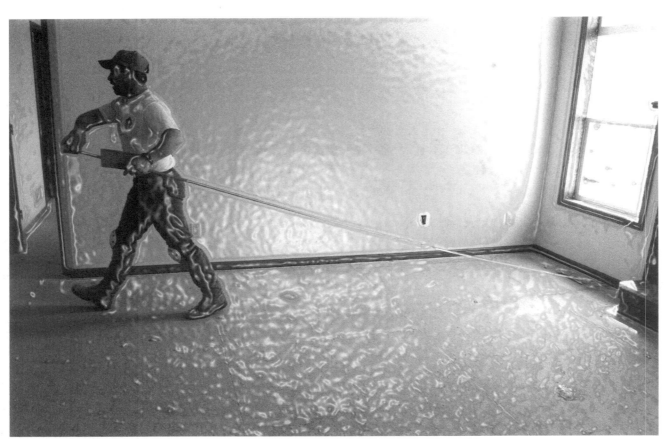

Art work: © 2002 Eric M. Larson

The bitterness of poor quality lingers long after the sweetness of a bargain is forgotten.

Although I'm sure you are eager to jump in and start installing your carpet, first you must acquire accurate measurements to figure the correct yardage and/or square feet.

You will need a few things in order to obtain correct measurements and layout for the carpet. You will need some **drafting paper** with square grids on it to draw the schematic drawing and a **pencil**. The square grids are used to draw out the balance piece and accurately figure the fills. Each grid is equal to one foot. You will also need a **30 foot steel tape measure** and a **calculator**.

If you think that measuring for carpet involves measuring from wall to wall and then multiplying them together for the square feet of carpet that you will need, you will be sorely short on carpet 90% of the time.

For instance with a ten by ten bedroom you would be two foot short of the wall. Carpet comes in a standard width of 12 foot wide and does not fit the room without waste.

If you could melt the carpet down and pour it into the room then this method would work.

DRAWING THE SCHEMATIC

First you will draw a schematic drawing of the areas to be carpeted so that you can see the best layout for the job and have a record of the correct measurements, the seam placements, and other valuable observations to take note of. In the drawing include all corners. Write down the measurements for all areas small and large. *Your drawing does not have to be 100% perfectly correct in size but your measurements do.* The schematic drawing includes:

• **The customers name & address & phone #, date of installation.**
• **The correct measurements, plus 4 inches extra on each cut, for 2 inches extra up each wall.**
• **The carpet cuts (measurements) for each area.**
• **The width of the carpet. (12 -foot wide, 13 ft. 6 inches, or 15 ft. wide.)**
• **The type of carpet being installed. (Berber, plush, commercial, woven.)**
• **The correct yardage or square feet needed.**
• **The notes of observations (see section below)**
• **Width and length of the steps.**
• **The placement of seams, correctly figured carpet needed for seams, and additional carpet added for pattern matches on every seam.**

THE LAYOUT

The layout is the direction that you run the carpet and the placement of seams. You need to decide on the layout of the carpet before you can figure the correct yardage and cuts needed for each room. You need to know the width of the carpet in order to decide the best direction to run the carpet.

1. You run the carpet in the direction that has the least number and feet of seams.

2. You lay the carpet so that the seams are out of direct traffic as much as possible.

3. You lay the carpet so that you use the least amount of carpet.

4. You can not always achieve all of these objectives but they are your objectives. Decide what is most important to you and the customer.

Installing the carpet with the least number and feet of seams is most often the best layout. This can in some cases increase the total square feet of carpet needed. This would depend on the layout of the particular job.

All carpet of the same type (color and dye lot) are run in the same direction. *You may run carpets in different areas, that are not directly connected by seams, in a different direction.* You might do this if you are carpeting the bedrooms and not the hallway, if it would allow a room to drop with no seams. This would not be applicable if there is a pattern in the carpet that makes this noticeable.

RULES OF MEASURING

Once you have a schematic drawing made you are ready to take the measurements.

1. Measure the largest area of the room. ***Through the doors***, not from wall to wall. Measure ***over the top step***, not to the top edge of the step.

2. Add two inches extra to go up each wall. This is 4 inches extra over the exact measurement. You need this to stretch and trim the carpet properly. If the carpet is flush against the wall it will bind when stretching. The trimmer does not trim properly with less than 1 inch of carpet. Rooms are not always exactly square, and the carpet can also shift out of place slightly when stretching, this must be considered when adding extra on the cuts.

3. The edge of the carpet for seams is trimmed off, so figure 2 inches extra for the width of each area with seam. Figure the width of each seam, and round this out to the next highest number that divides evenly into the width of the carpet used. Divide the length of the seam by the number that you found divides evenly into the carpet width.

4. If you order a full roll from the mill the last several feet may be damaged, take this into consideration when ordering.

5. Carpet with a pattern match requires extra carpet, know this amount and add for it *for each*

seam area.

6. Measure the width of the steps, round this out to the next higher number that will divide into twelve evenly. The carpet is installed with the nap (pile) laying down over the step, not sideways (quarter turned).

7. Measure down the total length of the steps, pushing the tape measure into each step. Add an extra foot to the total length down steps. When installing the carpet on the steps the carpet will not always complete the last step and this carpet is wasted, this is why an extra foot is needed.

MISTAKES OF MEASURING

1. Measuring a hallway from wall to wall and not through each doorway. Most doorways have seams or rolled edge that require extra carpet. When a hallway is to be seamed in pieces the width must be rounded out to the next highest amount that will divide into the width of carpet being used. A 4'6 wide hall is rounded out to 6'.

2. Not adding 4 inches extra to the exact measurement, to allow 2 inches up each wall for stretching and trimming.

3. Not measuring for closets, thinking that all of the scraps can be seamed up for closets.

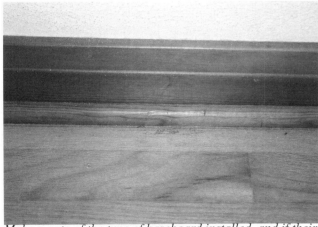

Make a note of the type of baseboard installed, and if their is quarter round installed. Pictured is baseboard with quarter round installed, a low and rounded quarter round should be removed for carpet installation. The warranty for the carpet staying tucked is voided if it is not removed.

4. Not adding extra for seams. Not rounding out the width on seams to the next highest number that will divide evenly into the width of carpet used. Not adding extra for the inch that is cut off of each seam piece.

5. Not measuring for steps. Not pushing the tape measure down into each step tread for an accurate measurement. Not rounding out the width on steps to the next highest number that will divide evenly into the width of carpet used. Not adding 1 foot extra on to the total length down steps.

6. Not adding for a pattern match on **every** seam area.

7. Thinking that you can stretch 2 inches out of the carpet. (You can't).

OBSERVATIONS OF THE ROOM

As you are drawing the schematic drawing and measuring, you are observing the area and taking note of the following conditions:

What type of baseboards are installed? Raised, flat on the floor, with quarter round etc. Is their old floor covering to be removed and is it stretched in or glued direct?

How many feet of metals will be needed?

Is there furniture and/or appliances to be moved? Is there anything on the walls that needs to be removed before installation?

Look to see a good route for carrying the carpet into the house.

If no floor covering is down, are there any repairs that need to be made to the floor and what condition is the tack strip in?

If there are steps what type are they? (See section IV)

Is there construction work that needs to be done for carpet to be installed properly, ledges that carpet wraps over that needs a piece of wood for the carpet to wrap under. Steps that are not constructed properly.

Are there any additional charges that may apply? Radiator heaters, posts, carpet tear out, upholstered steps, bullnosed steps, wrap around steps, quarter round, and tack strip that need to

be removed.

Tack strip that is in *good condition* (**not** rotting with the pins rusted off), should be left in place, but, if there is quarter round to be removed then the tack strip must also be removed, because the tack strip would be to far away from the wall.

If the baseboards are installed over the tack strip, either the baseboards need to be removed, or the tack strip needs to be removed and reinstalled.

The tack strip must be the proper distance from the wall, 3/8th of and inch, or it must be removed and reinstalled.

Carpet can be installed with baseboards off or with them on. If new baseboards are being installed first, they should be installed 3/8th to 1/2 of an inch off of the floor. This allows for the carpet to be tucked more smoothly.

Pictured measuring for carpet. Measure accurately and add four inches to each measurement, to allow two inches up each wall. Always measure the largest area of the room.

ARE THERE ANY CONSTRUCTION PROBLEMS OF THE HOME?

The best time to notice any problems with the house is in advance so that they can be corrected prior to installing the carpet.

Examples:

Floor damage due to termites or water damage. **Side running boards on steps** that are to **low** so that the raw edge of carpet will show. A **water leak** that wasn't noticed prior to removing the carpet such as a toilet leaking.

Carpet that wraps over a ledge and does not have a board attached to wrap the carpet around and staple it under. In other words, the wall that the carpet is to be wrapped over is made of dry wall, and the previous carpet was turned under and stapled. This is **not the correct way** to achieve a quality look.

CONVERTING INCHES TO DECIMAL POINTS

In order to add all of your room cuts together, and calculate the total number of feet of carpet needed for the job, you will need to convert the inches to decimals.

It may make it easier to add, *if you round out the measurement to the next highest, even decimal point:* 3 inches - .25, 6 inches - .50, 9 inches - .75. This is so the cuts add up more easily.

1 inch = .08
2 inches = .17
3 inches = .25
4 inches = .334
5 inches = .42
6 inches = .50
7 inches = .58
8 inches = .6
9 inches = .75
10 inches = .83
11 inches. = .92

An example of adding cuts with the decimal points for inches:

15.25
12.75
25.25
13.50
66.75 Total feet

FOOT TO YARD CONVERSION

Carpet is sold by the square foot but sometimes you need to know the square yards. Some installers charge by the square yard. This is a simple conversion:

Method One: Foot to yard conversion.
If the carpet is 12 feet wide multiply the length by : 1.334
If the carpet is 13 feet 6 inches wide, multiply the length by : 1.50
If the carpet is 15 feet wide multiply the length by : 1.67

For example if you have a 12 foot wide carpet 66.75 feet long multiply 66.75 x 1.334 = 89.04 yards. This is the fastest method.

Method Two: Foot to yard conversion.
You can also achieve this by multiplying the length of the carpet needed by the width that the carpet came, then divide the total square feet by nine to come up with the square yards.

Examples # 1: 66.75 feet x 12 ft. wide carpet = 801 square feet, divided that by 9 = 89 yards. This is a bit longer method than the first.

Example # 2: 15 ft. wide carpet x 100 ft. = 1500 sq feet, divided by 9 = 166.66 sq yards.

FOUR COMMON LAYOUTS

Lets do an exercise and I will walk you through figuring the carpet for these four layouts. **The first layout is a bedroom.** This is a common layout. The second is of a **large open living room.** The third is an **L shaped living room and dinning room.** The fourth layout is a

Layout # 1
The Layout of a BedRoom

12' wide carpet
Cuts

17'3"
x 12
= 207 sq ft
divided by 9 = **23 yards**

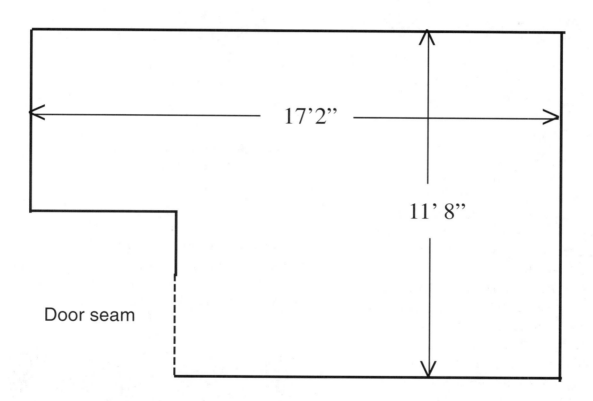

17'2"

11' 8"

Door seam

Notes
No door metals
Remove old floor Covering (stretch in carpet)
Baseboards - flat on the floor
Tack strip is rotting and must be replaced
Wood floor
No furniture in the room

seam = ----------

hallway and three bedrooms. This is the largest layout that you will figure. So get out your calculator and let's figure carpet!

LAYOUT # 1
A BEDROOM

First notice that **the room is less than 12 foot wide** so your *carpet will drop with no seams*. The longest area is 17' feet 2". The actual room length should be 4 inches less, being that you added 4 inches to the exact measurement. I then rounded this out to 3, a decimal point of .25 for easier adding. The measurement that you write down is the size that the carpet will be cut.

To figure the yardage look at the inch to decimal conversion chart, then look at the foot to yard conversion chart. The carpet is 12 feet wide so multiply 17.25 x 1.334 = 23 yards. Take a look at the notes that are taken for the bedroom.

LAYOUT TWO
A LIVING ROOM

On this layout the room is 15 foot 3 inches by 27 feet long, so you will need to have a seam. You want to place the seam out of the traffic as much as possible without wasting carpet. **Remember the seam carpet runs the same direction as the rest of the room**. The width of the seam area is *over* **3 foot wide**, you will round this out to the next highest number that divides into 12 evenly, (four foot.) The carpet you will use for the seam is *12 foot wide* and *four* divides into 12 **three** times evenly. **Three** is the number you will divide the length of the seam by .

To figure the carpet you will need for the seam, divide the total length of the seam area (27 feet) by **three**. You will be cutting several inches off for seam edges.

This gives you a 9 foot long x 12 wide piece for the seam and it will be done in three pieces. You must cut one inch off of each edge for cross seams so add four inches extra, giving you a 9 foot 4" piece. You may want to round this out to an even decimal for adding.

If you are figuring a large job with many seams, you will figure each seam as you did this one, but you will add together the total of the carpet for **all seams** and leave it on one piece of carpet (*the balance*). This will give you a longer piece of carpet, so that you will have less cross seams. You can add extra to this **(balance)** amount *if* you only need several feet more in order to drop all of the seams in one piece.

What if you had miss measured this job and measured the width at under 15 wide? What would this do to you? The seam width would then only be three foot wide instead of four; so three divides into 12 **four** times instead of **three** as we just figured, now you would divide the total length of the seam (27') by **four** thinking that you can make the seam in four pieces instead of three, and you can't! *You would than order a 6.75 piece for the seam instead of the 9' piece that you need.* You can see how miss measuring by three inches can make you short on carpet.

LAYOUT # THREE
A LIVING ROOM & DINNING ROOM

On this layout the length of 23 ft. 6" is less than two 12 foot carpet rolls, (24 ft.) so you can run the carpet in this direction with the least seams. If the carpet width was 15 feet wide you could run it the other direction with even fewer seams. You will have two cuts 13.75 ft. and 30 ft. add them together = 43.75 x 1.334 = 58.25

A room ready to measure notice the post in the middle of the room when measuring. Take note of this, this may need to be seamed for the carpet to go around them, and require more work.

Layout # 2
The Layout of a Living Room

12' wide carpet
Cuts
27' for the main area
<u>+ 9'6" for the seam</u>
= 36'6" ft.
36.50 x 1.334
= 48.69 yards

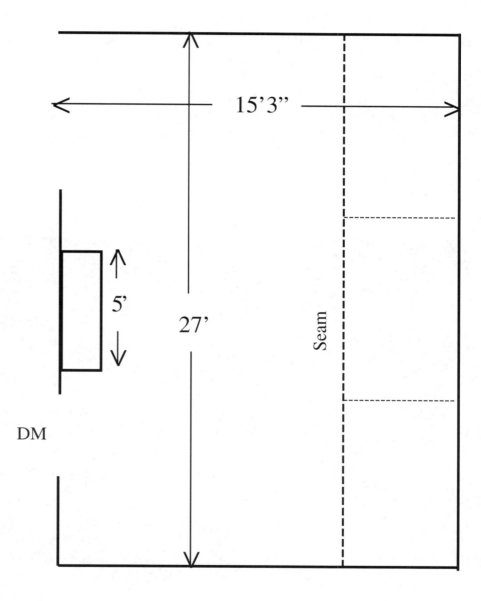

15'3"

27'

5'

Seam

DM

Notes
No baseboards installed (install after installation)
No furniture
Tack strip is in good condition, and the correct distance
from the walls.
9' door metals needed
Concrete floor

seams = ----------

yards. 12 x 43.75 = 525 sq ft.

If you were using a 15 wide carpet you would multiply by 1.67 to achieve the yardage. Take a look at the notes: you will need 8 feet of metals and there is an entry door and a kitchen door that most likely have vinyl. Observe the room and take notes of the type of baseboard, how many feet of metals you will need, the width of the carpet you will install, if there is a pattern match, the type of floor covering that is installed and if you will be removing it; also take note of any posts or rails to go around.

Take a look at the notes on layout # 3: you will be taking notes of observations for all of the jobs that you measure.

MEASURING LAYOUT FOUR
A HALL & THREE BEDROOMS

This layout appears rather complicated at first look but it's not. Take it one step at a time and its no different than the other layouts.

I'll walk you through the whole layout as you do the adding and multiplying. All of the carpet is 12 feet wide. Write the cuts for each room down separately. The MBR is 19 feet. The MBR closet is 6 foot. BR # 2 is 15 foot. BR # 1 is 12 foot 4 inches.

Pictured is a railing with posts to go around and a ledge to carpet over. This is a situation that must be observed and the options discussed with the customer. Never turn and tack (turn the edge under and staple or nail the carpet directly to dry wall on a ledge) Always nail a 2 x 4 to the wall to wrap the carpet around and staple underneath or use a metal as is shown. Extra charges apply for extra labor such as railings with posts and ledges to wrap over. Installing wood for these ledges is an extra labor charge by the installer and the customer must be aware of this.

Layout # 3
The Layout of a living Room & Dinning Room

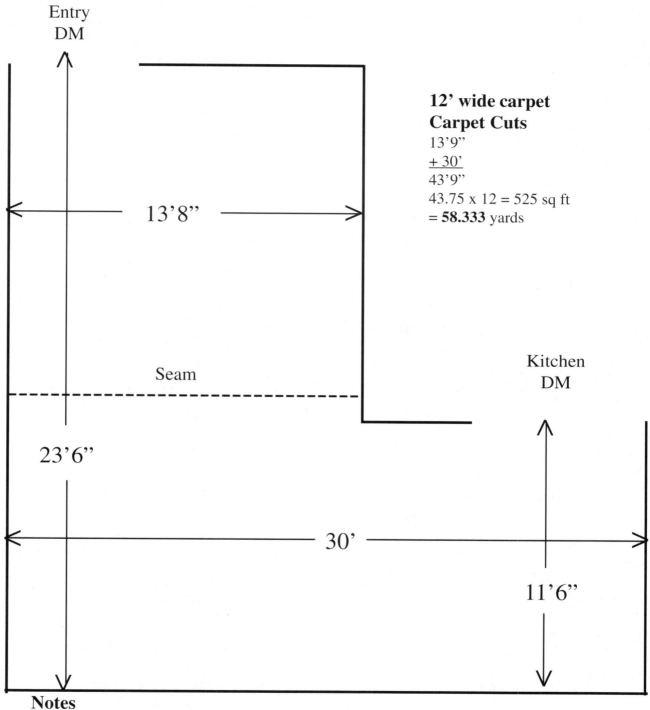

Entry
DM

12' wide carpet
Carpet Cuts
13'9"
+ 30'
43'9"
43.75 x 12 = 525 sq ft
= **58.333** yards

13'8"

Seam

Kitchen
DM

23'6"

30'

11'6"

Notes
8' of Door metals
No floorcovering down
Quarter round installed, the customer will
remove
No tack strip is installed
No furniture

seam = ------------

FIGURING SEAMS ON LARGE JOBS

Each seam is figured separately, this is the only accurate method to acquire correct carpet yardage. To figure how much carpet you need for a seam you **divide** the **seams length**. The number that you divide the **length** by is determined by the **width** of the seam area.

I will use layout # 4 for this example. The carpet is 12 foot wide, and all rooms are 14 feet 6 wide, this means that the seam width, (the width of the carpet needed for the seam area) is 2 feet 6 inches in **all rooms**. Round this out to three foot, because 3 divides into twelve evenly 4 times. **Four is the number that you divide the length of all the seams by,** to acquire the carpet amount for that seam.

Divide each of the room seam lengths. **BR # 1** has a 12 ft. 4" long seam area so let's round it out to 13 to allow a little extra. It's always better to add some extra inches than to be short on carpet. Divide 13 by 4 = 3 ft. 3 inches for BR #1 seam. **BR # 2** is 15 ft. long, divide 15.50 by 4 = 3.875 Round this up to four foot even for BR # 2 seam. The **MBR** is 19 feet and the **closet** is 6 feet 6. Add this together for 25.50 divided by 4 = 6.37. Round up to 6 foot 6 inches for the MBR & closet seam.

FIGURING THE HALLWAY

The hallway is 5 ft. wide. Five will divide into 12 twice, so divide the length of the hall by 2 = 9 foot 6 inches for the hall. I will add 3 inches to this for 9' 9 inches for the hall. The hallway and seam pieces are figured separately like this, (because it's the most accurate method) but they're not cut because if they're left on one piece, then all of the seams and hallway are in one piece. That makes for less seams!

Now you add all of these cuts to come up with **the balance**; this is left on one piece so that the seams can drop without cross seams.

12' Wide Carpet
Add the balance (The balance is the pieces figured for seams and hallway added together.)

Hallway - 9'.75" -
Bedroom # 1 - 3'.25"
Bedroom # 2 - 4'.00"
Master bedroom - 6'.50"
= 23'.50'' total balance

Now total all of the cuts for every thing and then figure the yardage.

Add all cuts (Bedrooms & master br closet)

$$
\begin{array}{ll}
23'.50'' & \text{balance} \\
19'.00'' & \text{MBR} \\
6'.6'' & \text{Closet} \\
15'.00'' & \text{BR \#2} \\
+12'.50'' & \text{BR \#1} \\
\hline
76.50' \times 1.334 & \\
\end{array}
$$
= 102 yards
76.50 x 12 = 918 sq ft.

The total yardage is **102,** *the total square feet is 918 sq ft.* That is the amount of carpet needed for this job.

BALANCE SHEET

The smaller pieces are all left on one piece called the **balance**, this is so the seams and hallways can be done in one piece. You figure each seam and hallway as a separate piece, but then total them together for the *balance sheet.* Draw the amount of carpet you figured for the *balance* on a sheet of drafting paper with square grids, to figure the seam, and hallway pieces accurately. Each grid is equal to one foot. If you need one or two more feet of carpet for a seam to drop, without a cross seam, you can add one or more feet, *with the customers permission.*

The balance is the hall the closets and all the seams in this case. We figured each separately for accuracy, on a larger job, such as this one, these amounts are all left on one piece of carpet, known as *the balance.* This require less

Layout # 4
The Layout of a Hall & Three Bed Rooms

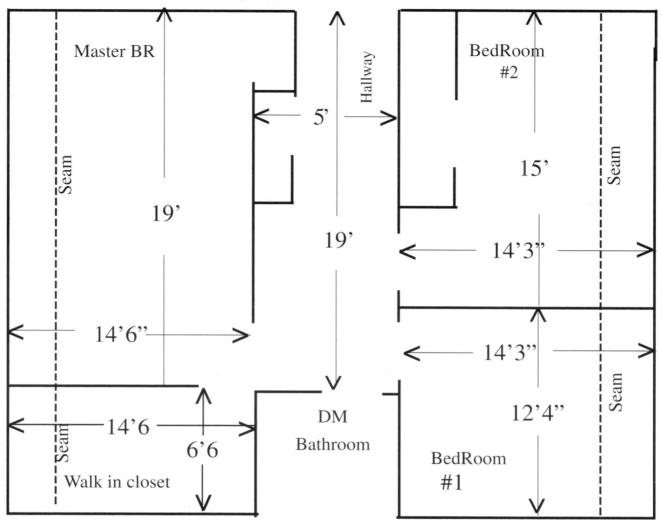

Notes

   Installer to remove old floor covering, stretch in carpet is installed.
   Baseboards are raised
   No furniture
   3' door metals

seam = -------------------

Cuts -   12' Wide Carpet
Master bedroom **19'**
 closet **6'6"**
 BR #2 **15'**
 BR#1 **12'6"**

Balance (The hall, seams, and
 small closet is the balance) - leave
these on one piece - **23.50 x 12**
 Hallway   9'6" on balance
 Seam BR #1   3'6" on balance
 Seam BR #2   4' on balance
 Master BR & closet seams 6'6" on balance

Total Feet = 76.50 x 12 = **918 sq feet**
918 sq feet divided by 9 = **102 sq yards**

Layout #4
Carpet Balance Sheet

Balance (The hall, seams, and small closet is the balance) - leave these on one piece:

    Hallway   **9'9"** on balance
    Seam BR #1   **3'3"** on balance
    Seam BR #2   **4'** on balance
    Master BR & closet seams **6'6"** on balance

Balance Total = 23.50 x 12

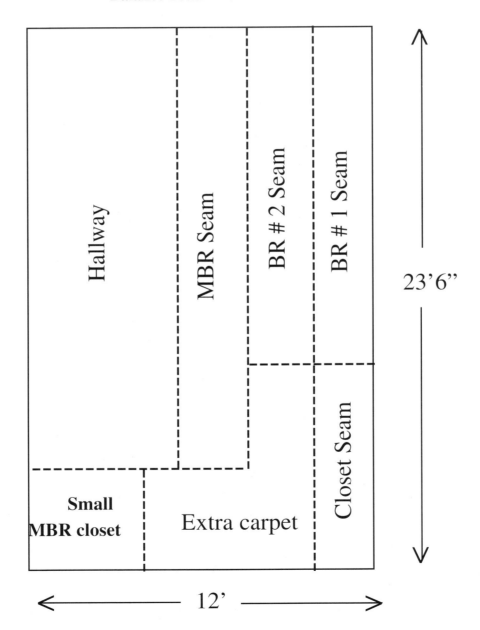

work seaming, because the seams are all in one piece, with out cross seams. It also makes for a better quality of job with less chance of a problem from seams. On a larger job like this one I like to draw the balance out on drafting paper having each grid represent one foot. It makes it a lot easier when you can see how the cuts will be taken out of the carpet. As you can see, all of the seams and the hallway will be in one piece without any cross seams. There will be a small amount of extra carpet left, but it's better to have a little extra than not enough. **Less seams mean less chance for a problem, and less work seaming for you.**

MEASURING STEPS

You measure the width of the steps and round this out to the next higher amount that divides into the width of the carpet you are using, (normally 12 ft. wide carpet). If the step measures 3' 3 inches, this would round out to four feet, if they measured 4' 8 inches, this would round out to 6 feet. If the step is four feet wide and the carpet is 12, four will divide into 12, three times. The steps would then be done in three pieces.. **Divide the length of the steps by this number.**

Measure down the length of the steps, pushing the tape measure tight to the steps, and holding it into place. **Add one foot to the total length measurement**, two for bullnosed steps (steps stapled under the lip).This is because the steps are not done in one continuouse pieces of carpet, so the last piece used is not always large enough to finish a step.

The nap (pile) always runs down the step, not sideways. Running the carpet sideways (quarter turned) can leave a gap along the walls on the steps.

MEASURING FOR A CUSTOMER

The first impression that the customer will have of you is when you come to measure for the carpet, *and the first impression is a lasting impression.* Be polite and professional, dress clean, and be sensitive to the customers questions and concerns.

Make sure to come to an agreement as to who is to tear up and haul away the old carpet, and who is to move furniture and appliances.

If appliances have gas orwater lines, arrangements need to be made for a service man to disconnect and reconnect them. You place yourself at great risk of liability if you do this yourself, and have a leak.

THE BASIC INSTALLATION IN-CLUDES

1. Measuring for the correct layout and yardage of carpet needed.

2. Delivering the carpet and pad with an installation.

3. Installation of tack strips and metals.

4. Sweeping the floor.

5. Complete installation of the carpet.

6. Some installers vacuum the carpet.

7. Some installers wipe down the woodwork to remove scuffs.

5. A one year warranty of the carpet installation.

EXTRA COSTS ABOVE THE BASIC

Extra charges that may apply. Example: Removing and / or hauling away old carpet and pad, steps (bullnosing steps, pie steps, capped ends.) Upholstery work, rolled edges. Floor prep work (example: floor patching, tearing up tack strip, tearing up 1/4 round, floor disinfecting.) Installing around posts, toilets, steam heat units, claw foot bathtubs, furniture and appliance moving. Installation includes floor sweeping, but excessive clean up is extra.

CUSTOMER HANDOUT SHEET

INSTALLATION BASICS

1. Have placement of seams been discussed with you?

2. Any low hanging items in closets should be removed. (dresses, coats, shelves.)

3. Tack strip should **not** be removed unless it is rotten.

4. Any doors opening into the area to be installed must be removed.

5. If the new carpet and pad are thicker than the old you may have to trim the doors.

6. All areas that are to be carpeted must be completely empty.

7. Quarter round should be removed to stretch and tuck carpet properly. If it is not removed this could void the warranty for the carpet staying tucked and stretched tightly.

8. Do you understand that extra charges may apply? Example: Removing and / or hauling away old carpet and pad, steps (bullnosing steps, pie steps, capped ends.) Upholstery work, rolled edges. Floor prep work (example: floor patching, tearing up tack strip, tearing up 1/4 round, floor disinfecting.) Installing around posts, toilets, steam heat units, claw foot bathtubs, furniture and appliance moving.

9. If new baseboard's are to be installed they should be raised 1/2 inch off the floor.

10. Anything that could be knocked off of the walls or shelves should be removed.

11. You may need to touch up paint and baseboard's due to the coarseness of the carpet backing.

12. Carpet and pad that is to be hauled away by us is to be rolled up in 4' wide rolls and placed near the driveway.

13. Carpet and pad that is left balled up in the center of the room **is not removed.** The full price for removal will be charged in this case.

14. The floor should be swept and clean of pad prior to new installation.

15. When the customer removes the old floor covering (or their is no floor covering) they are responsible for having the floor clean and ready for installation. When we remove the old floor covering it is our responsibility to clean the floor. If clean up is not done we will charge for house cleaning.

PESTICIDE WARNING
Do not spray any pesticides prior to installation. We will be working along the walls and these products are neurological poisons that absorb through the skin!

1 YEAR INSTALLATION WARRANTY

Guarantees carpet to stay tucked along the walls and to stay in the metals provided by the installer.

Guarantees carpet to stay stretched tightly as not to wrinkle.

Guarantees seams to stay together.

Does not guarantee that seams are invisible.

There is no guarantee that wood work and paint will not be scuffed.

CHARGEABLE REPAIRS

Restretching carpet that has been pulled off of the tack strip by contractors or customers. Restretching due to flood damage. Patching carpet stains and burns.

QUIZ - THE FIRST PROCEDURE OF INSTALLATION
Measuring For Carpet

T/F 1. •You run the carpet in the direction that has the least number and feet of seams.

•You lay the carpet so that the seams are out of direct traffic as much as possible.

•You lay the carpet so that you use the least amount of carpet.

You can not always achieve all of these objectives but they are your objectives.

T/F 2. Carpet stretches several inches, so it's not neccesary to have the carpet up the walls, it would only waste carpet and money.

T/F 3. Measure down the total length of the steps, pushing the tape measure into each step. Add an extra foot to the total length down steps. When installing the carpet on the steps the carpet will not always complete the last step and this carpet is wasted. That is why an extra foot is needed.

T/F 4. Their is no need to measure steps or closets because all of the the scraps left over will be enough to do these areas.

T/F 5. Measure the largest area of the room. *Through the doors*, not from wall to wall. Measure *over the top step*, not to the top edge of the step.

T/F 6. Carpet with a pattern match requires extra carpet, add for the pattern match, know this amount and add for it.

T/F 7. If there are seams, the edge of the carpet for seams is trimmed off, so figure 2 inches extra for the width of each area with seam. Figure the width of each seam and round this out to the next highest number that divides evenly into twelve.

T/F 8. The smaller pieces are all left on one piece called the **balance**, this is so that the seams and hallways can be done in one piece. You figure each seam and hallway as a separate piece, but than total them together for the *balance sheet*.

T/F 9. The first impression that the customer will have of you is when you come to measure the carpet and the first impression is a lasting impression.

T/F 10. In order to add all of your room cuts together and calculate the total number of feet of carpet needed for the job you will need to convert the inches to decimals.

T/F 11. If you are working with a 12 ft. wide carpet, and the room in 15 ft. 3 in. wide, you can figure the seam width at 3 ft wide, and 3 divides into twelve 4 times. So to find the correct amount of carpet for the seam divide the length of the seam by 4.

T/F 12. As you are drawing the schematic drawing and measuring, you are observing the area and taking note of the following conditions:

What type of base boards are installed? Raised, flat on the floor, with quarter round etc.

Is there old floor covering to be removed, and is it stretched in or glued direct?

T/F 13. Quarter round should be removed to stretch and tuck carpet properly. If it is not removed this could void the warranty for the carpet staying tucked and stretched tightly.

T/F 14. It is not neccecary to remove any pictures or other breakable items from the walls for carpet installation.

T/F 15. You may need to touch up paint and baseboards due to the coarseness of the carpet backing.

T/F 16. The carpet on steps can be turned any direction and still look good.

Answers - 1. T 2. F 3. T 4. F 5. T 6. T 7. T 8. T 9. T 10. T 11. F 12.T 13. T 14. F 15.T 16.F

Pictured is a fork lift removing a roll of carpet from shelfs in a carpet store warehouse.

SECTION 2
THE PROCEDURES OF INSTALLATION

STEP ONE
CUTTING AND LOADING THE CARPET

A forklift removing the carpet roll from high shelves in a warehouse. A forklift is used to move and load all of the rolls of carpet in carpet stores.

Large rolls of carpet are removed from shelves in the warehouse, or from stacks of carpet in the carpet store, by a **forklift**. *The large roll is cut to the specific lengths of each room for the house* in the warehouse. There usually is not any place to cut the carpet at the job site. It is also very heavy and difficult to handle.

Cutting carpet on sight is called field cutting. You are subject to adverse weather conditions, and difficult cutting locations not to mention a large and very heavy roll of carpet to move around if you use this method. The carpet is subject to becoming dirty, wet and stained. Typical field cutting locations are parking lots, driveways, lawns and garages.

Cutting the carpet to the various room sizes at the warehouse is the preferred method. You will probably be forced to field cut

Here is a full van load of carpet on a winter day. Unless you use an extended van you will have carpet hanging out of the back. Purchase some bungie cords to tie the back doors shut and place a red flag on the roll sticking out the farthest.

Removing the wrapping from the carpet roll prior to pulling it out across the warehouse in order to make the cuts for each room. The wrapping protects the carpet when being transported to carpet stores across the country and in the warehouse when being stored.

The carpet is being pulled out across the floor so that it can be measured and cut to the lengths needed for each room in the house.

The carpet is measured then a small cut is make along the edge of both sides to mark it. Use a chalk line to mark all the way across.

Use a stand up carpet cutter to cut the carpet.

carpet from time to time by carpet stores with inadequate space, or just poor management.

The jobs are pre-measured and a schematic drawing made, so that the cuts for each room are already known. *The schematic drawing is essential for referring back to on the layout plan of the house.* Measure accurately using the cut list you've made on the job site. Cut a small mark in the side to the lengths needed, then mark the carpet using a chalk line. Now you can cut each piece.

Roll up each piece of carpet the *same* direction so that when it is laid out in the house the carpet is all going the *same* direction. **Write the length of each piece**, on the *same* corner of the backing of each roll. The writing on each corner also insures that you have laid out each

piece the same direction in the house.

When you get the carpet into the house, you can *check that the corner marked is on the same corner through out the house* by folding back each corner. This helps to guarantee that all of the carpet is laid out the same direction throughout the house. If there are a lot of pieces, then you have to mark the size on the corner so that you know which one goes in each room.

Never roll up one piece from one direction and the next from the other. You will have them going in opposite directions.

Load the large carpet rolls onto the van with a forklift to save your strength, you will be carrying it into the house by hand later, and will need this energy.

Each piece of carpet is rolled up the same direction so that when it is rolled out in the house it is all going the same direction. The nap must lay the same direction through the house.

Mark each corner on the same end of the rolls with its size.

Load the carpet on to the van using the fork lift.

Pushing the remaining amount of carpet into the van by hand. The fork lift can not always load it all of the way in. Make sure that you have enough pad and supplies on the van before leaving for the job.

STEP TWO
CARRYING IN TOOLS AND SUPPLIES

Carrying in tools and supplies is a big part of a carpet job. **Be very careful not to scrape anything with your tool boxes** as you enter and carry them through the house. Watching out for door jams, doors, and walls is essential when carrying in tools.

You may want to **prop the front door open,** so that you can more easily get into the house or building while carrying in tools and supplies.

Be as **efficient in your trips as possible.**

Pictured is a machine that cuts and rolls the carpet without using up a lot of space in the warehouse. The cuts needed are punched into the machines digital cut programer, and it makes the cuts and rolls the carpet.

If there are not a lot of steps, a dolly can carry in all of your tools in one trip.

Load all of your tools on the dolly, it will save many trips of hand carrying.

You can still use a dolly if there are steps, but it is not advisable if there are a large number of steps.

The dolly in the house can be used as a cart to keep the tool boxes off of the floor.

*Carrying the main tool box and seam box into the house.
The main tool box is needed for every job. If seams are
being done then the seam box will be needed.*

*Prop open the front door of the house when carrying in
tools, pad, carpet and other supplys. Be very careful not
to scrape the walls or door jams when carrying in.*

Make the most of each trip out to the van. Don't carry in unnecessary items that are not needed for the particular job. Carry as much as you can safely handle on each trip.

I've recently been using a two wheel dolly to carry in all of my tool. It's been a huge time saver.

Set all tools in an area **out of the work area** (area to be carpeted). Carpet and pad can not be installed if your tools are in the way and you will have to keep moving them all the time. **Do not** set tools in the **middle of the room** where you'll have to keep moving them all of the time. Set them in an area as *close* to where you

are working as possible but *not* where the carpet is being installed.

Set a rug, piece of cardboard, pad, or carpet scrap **under the tools** to **protect the floor** if it is a sensitive material that will scratch. Treat other people's homes as you would your own.

STEP THREE
REMOVE ANY DOORS OPENING INTO THE AREA.

Doors that open into the area where the carpet is to be installed should be removed. It is impossible to install carpet and pad with doors on.

Use a pry bar, nail, or specific pin removing tool with a hammer to **remove the pins from the hinges on the doors**. Be careful not to scratch the wood on the doors, or the hinges

Carrying in the power stretcher and extra tube boxes,

*Carrying in a twelve foot metal and the tack strip. Carry in
any supplies needed for the job! Are metals needed for the
job? Is tack strip needed?*

Tools that are set out of the way in the kitchen. Always set tools off of the floor that is being carpeted. Place something on the floor to protect it from the tool boxes.

Carrying in an older style of power stretcher in a wood box. For a stretch - in job the power stretcher is always needed. If the carpet is being glued direct than you wouldn't need a power stretcher.

themselves. A nail may pose less risk of scratching the hinge than a pry bar.

When you are **carrying doors** that have been removed, watch so that you do not bang into any walls with the corner of the door. Take your time. Doors can be awkward to carry; grip it in both hands and **tilt the top downward**. Sometimes they can be carried with the **top tilted slightly sideways** without hitting the ceiling.

Doors that open into areas that are **not** being carpeted, **do not** need to be removed. For example, a door opening into a bathroom does

not need to be removed to carpet the hallway, unless you are also carpeting the bathroom.

Once the door is removed set it out of the way but **as close as possible to the area from where you removed the door.** Remove all of the doors from the area that is being carpeted.

MARKING DOORS

If you are **removing a lot of doors** you will need a method to remember which ones went where. You can **organize the pins differently in each door**, for example, in one door leave the pins in the door jam, in another leave the pins in the door hinges themselves, in another leave one pin in the door and one in the door jam.

Another method is to **use a pencil and write a number on each door hinge and door jam hinge**. If your only removing a few doors all of this is not necessary, you can remember which ones go where by memory.

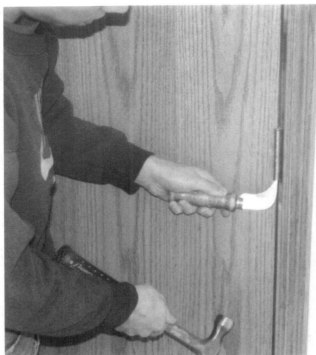

Remove a door using a tucker or pry bar and a hammer. A nail can also be used to push the pins up. Their is also a specific tool for removing door pins available at floor covering supply stores.

The door pins are being removed after pushing them up with a tucker.

Do not write on the hinges with a permanent marker or any marker for that matter, only use a pencil. Place pieces of cardboard, or pad on the floor and the wall to protect the walls from being scratched.

Place doors, if possible, **as close to the door jam that they were removed from**. If you remove a door from the living room closet, place it in the kitchen. This also helps you to remember where the door goes.

Doors are often **placed in bathrooms**, **kitchens**, and **entry ways** on large jobs. If a shortage of space occurs doors can be put in the garage or even outside.

If there was not any carpet installed previously or **the new carpet and pad are thicker than the old**, then the doors may be too low, and need to be **trimmed off**.

STEP FOUR
REMOVING THE OLD CARPET & PAD

The first step to removing the old floor covering is **removing the furniture**. You can not remove the old carpet with furniture on top of it, or install the new pad and carpet. All of **the furniture must be removed from the areas to be carpeted** . The furniture is put into areas that are *not* going to be carpeted, such as into the kitchen, garage, bedrooms, or even outside, if weather permits.

If their is to much furniture to move at once, you will install, and remove the carpet in phases, for example the living room, dinning room and hall would be installed on one day, and the bedrooms the next.

There is only **one exception to not removing** *all* **of the furniture** that I have come across. **A piece of furniture that can not reasonably be removed from the area,** because it was assembled in an area **without** adequate door sizes or storage space.

I have installed carpet in a basement with a slate pool table that could not be removed without disassembling it. It is an exception that some times has to be made, but requires additional techniques in stretching. It also requires a lot of extra work moving the piece around the room to install pad and carpet. Is this extra work more than the work of removing the piece of furniture?

There are many different types of carpet and pad removal. There is **stretch in carpet removal**, **direct glue** removal, direct glue with **kanga back**, **stapled down** removal, and **double glue** removal. There are also many different types of padding, that have different removal characteristics. Some pad types are foam, rebond, waffle, and horse hair.

Some homes did not have carpet previously, or the home is newly constructed, so removal is not necessary.

I recommend that **the old carpet is vacu-**

umed prior to having it removed. This will keep the dust and pollutants from being spread throughout the house and into the new carpet. It will help prevent allergies in prone individuals.

The most common carpet removal is stretch in. **To remove stretch in carpet,** first pull up along the walls to release the old carpet from the tack strip. Grip with your fingers or use pliers. Often times the corners pull up more easily than along the walls. Release all of the perimeter of the room from the tack strip.

Next, **fold back the carpet** and then cut it into strips three to four feet wide. **Cut from the backside** of the carpet not the nap (pile) side. Cutting from the top will dull your knife blade

Pictured are doors that have been removed and set inside the bathroom that is not to be carpeted.
Develop a system of marking doors so that you can remember where each door goes. Number the hinges with a pencil, arrange the door pins differently in each door, or put doors closer to the room that they were removed from. You can use a combination of these methods.

The door is being removed after the pins are taken out.

much faster. Smaller strips like this are more easily handled. Roll up the strips of carpet and lay them near the van. Remember, the van is full of the new carpet and pad so you can not load the old in yet.

Pulling up an entire carpet in one piece is unnecessary, unless it is going to be used by someone for reinstallation. **A two wheel dolly** can be used to wheel out large heavy rolls.

With two people working, one of you can start carrying out all of the old carpet and pad, as the other continues cutting and rolling up strips of carpet and pad.

During rainy weather conditions you'll have to keep the old carpet and pad in the garage, or covered because, it will get so heavy and soaked that it can not be lifted. You would also soak the van, when you load it to haul it away. It is important to keep the van clean, remember you also haul *new* carpet in it!

When removing the carpet in a hallway, if the bedroom carpet will not be replaced, cut the carpet so that you leave extra out into the hallway. This leaves extra for cutting the seams. Sometimes the seams were not made very well and they simply pull apart. **Do not cut into any areas that are not to be carpeted.**

Use a pry bar to remove the old metals, lay them outside with the old carpet. Be careful that nails are not dropped onto the driveway.

Observe the tack strip along the perimeter of the room and check its condition. Check under the windows and in front of entry ways. These are the areas that go bad first due to moisture. Bad pieces will look brown or black and the **pins will be rusting off**, give the piece a pull to see if the wood has any strength left. Pry up any pieces of the tack strip that are rotten, so that new can be installed.

The **stapled down pad** can be pulled loose from the staples or pad glue and rolled up. **Cut along the pad seams** that are taped together (rather than stapled) with duck tape. The standard width of pad is six foot wide so further cutting down of the size is not necessary.

Pieces of pad are often still stuck to the floor by the staples used to hold it in place when installing it. Remove any pieces of pad on the floor using the bottom of your shoe, a scraper, or pulling the staples with pliers. It is very important to remove these pieces, they can show bumps under the new carpet.

Removing staples is not always necessary. Pounding down any staples sticking up with a hammer, is often all that is needed. **Some installers may feel that it is necessary,** to pull all of the old staples. You will be adding more staples when you install the new pad, so as long as you can not feel any staples, it does not affect the quality of the installation.

Staples that are sticking up should be hammered down or removed, so that they are not felt through the carpet. Staples can be removed using pliers, or a scraper. Insert the scraper blade in backwards using the dull side to scrape with so that you don't damage the wood floor.

Clean used pad can be taken in to be recycled so do not roll up any tack strip or metals in with it. You will help the environment and also make some extra cash by recycling, so check with carpet supply stores on their recycling policy.

Glued down carpet is not so easy to remove, it is much harder to pull loose, and sometimes requires scraping pad off of the floor, such as with a kanga backed, and double glue carpet installations. Cut from the top so that the carpet pieces to pull up are smaller.

Kanga Back carpet that has been glued direct will leave the pad stuck to the floor and you will have to scrape it off. Kanga Back carpet has the pad attached directly to it and when you pull it up only the top comes up leaving the pad on the floor.

Use a razor blade scraper to scrape it up, not the short handled type but the type with a four foot handle. A tool like an ice scraper can also be used for scraping up pad. (See section 6) for more info on installing a kanga back carpet).

Double glue installation will also require scraping the pad off the floor, the pad is glued down first and then the carpet is glued down on top of the pad. It is most common on large commercial jobs. If you get into a large amount of pad to scrape up there is a **floor scraping machine** that you can rent or buy from a floor covering supply store.

STEP 5
CLEANING THE FLOOR

If you remove the old carpet and pad, you will need to sweep the floor thoroughly. Dirt from over the years will have built up in the carpet and worked its way through to the floor.

Foam pad often breaks down over the years and leaves a powder under the carpet. Normally all that is needed is to sweep the floor with a broom, or a shop vacuum.

After installing the tack strips and metals pick up any small pieces of tack strip or metal by hand. Sweep the entire room to make sure that no nails from installing the metals are left on the floor.

On a residential job you may arrive and the floor is whistle clean, if you don't have any metals or tack strip to install you won't need any further cleaning. **Cutting the tack strips** can leave splinters and small pieces that could be inadvertently left behind. It's best to make sure by sweeping, because it can be easy to roll the pad over a nail or piece of metal and not notice.

New construction will probably have more of a mess to clean up than residential homes. Saw dust, scraps of wood, and pieces of electrical wire will need to be swept up. Any joint compound from dry walling that is dried on the floor will need to be scraped off. You don't have to be quite as picky with stretch in carpet because the pad will cover and make any small bumps unnoticeable, but when you glue down a carpet direct you will need to be very careful to clean the floor thoroughly.

If a customer has a severe allergy to dust you will want to use a shop vacuum instead of a broom to keep the dust level down. Make sure you sweep up any nails that may have fallen out of the metals.

STEP 6
FLOOR PREP WORK

Floor Prep work is **anything done to the floor outside of a simple sweeping**. This would include floor patching of any holes or cracks in the floor. Leveling any uneven or higher areas in the floor. Removing quarter round, removing baseboards, moping and disinfecting the floor due to pet odors. It also could include repairing floors that are rotting due to water damage or termites. Floor prep work is above and beyond what is included in a basic installation.

DISINFECTING THE FLOOR

You don't want to install new carpet if any odors are absorbed into the floor. The new carpet won't cover it up, it's still going to be there and smell through to the new carpet.

To disinfect the floor and remove odors due to pets or water damage I mop the floor using a solution of Pine Sol and water. I mix a strong solution of 1 cup per gallon of Pine Sol with water. Mop the floor with a heavy solution being sure to get into the corners and along the walls. If the odors are soaked into the tack strip they will need to be torn up and replaced. Allow the solution to soak in and dry. I have had excellent results using this, even in very badly odorous homes. A light mix of bleach and water can also be used. Half of a cup mixed with one to two gallon of water is plenty.

Pictured sweeping the floor, a vacuum could also be used because this would raise less dust. Make sure there is not anything that could show a bump under the carpet. (Nails, Pieces of tack strip etc.)

Caution bleach will burn your skin and eyes, and reacts dangerously with ammonia. Follow the directions and cautions on the bottle.

FLOOR LEVELING

A **floor leveler** such as *Floor Stone* is used to level uneven floors. A floor that is higher in one area than another can be sloped so that there isn't a noticeable difference. Cracks and holes can be filled on a wood or concrete floor. Floor leveling is more vital on a glue direct carpet because there isn't any pad to cover the unevenness. **Floor Stone** is available as a dry mix prepared by mixing with latex. It sets up quickly so you don't want to mix such a large batch that you can not use it before it dries in the bucket.

FLOOR PATCHING

For a large patching area where the floor is rotten in certain areas, the bad areas will need to be cut out and replaced with new wood. A concrete floor that is in poor condition may need to be patched with concrete. **Removing the tack strip on concrete** will leave holes and if the tack strip is removed too often, eventually they will need patching, a good quality concrete should be used so that the masonry nails will hold. Floor Stone is not usable for nailing into but it's good for patching small holes in areas away from the wall.

Pictured is one possible floor disinfecting cause.

REMOVING QUARTER ROUND, TACK STRIP , and VINYL COVE BASE

Quarter round should be removed for carpet installation but it won't always be done. Some customers don't want it removed. Quarter round is originally installed to cover the edge on a wood floor. A low and rounded type of quarter round can be very difficult to stretch, trim and tuck carpet next to. No guarantee can be made as to the carpet staying tucked.

There is also a type of baseboard that is rounded at the bottom and must be removed.

Quarter round comes in many types, and a type that is higher and less rounded can sometimes be guaranteed.

Tack strip that is rotten, dried out, the pins are rusted off, or the incorrect space (gully) between the wall, (3/8th of and inch) needs to be removed. Pull on the strip to test its strength, and examine the pins. Remember you will *not* be able to stretch the carpet tightly with tack strip in poor shape. Also if the tack strip is not of a good quality, 1 inch wide or over, I often replace it.

Vinyl cove base is to be removed prior to installation and new, or the old base, reinstalled afterwards.

STEP SEVEN
INSTALLING TACK STRIP AND METALS

Prior to the invention and use of tackless strip, carpets were fastened to the floor using tacks, thus came the name *tackless* strip, since tacks were no longer used. The pins in the tack strip are as sharp as tacks and the name tackless strip no longer makes any sense to most people. Most installers refer to tackless strip as **tack strip**. Although it still says Tackless Strip on the box when you purchase it.

Grab a handful of tack strip being careful not to poke yourself with the sharp pins and **lay the pieces around the room with the pins facing the wall.** Position them around the perimeter of the room so they're ready to be nailed.

There are **two basic types of tack strip** *concrete* and *wood*. Tack strip comes pre nailed for wood and concrete. The only difference is the type of nails in them. The wood strip has longer narrower nails for nailing into a wood floor and the concrete has shorter, thicker nails (masonry nails). Masonry nails come in different sizes and lengths. You also use extra nails in areas that do not hold well, or do not have a nail due to cutting the strip.

Prior to installing the pad your knees are subjected to the most stress but I wear **knee pads through out the entire job, even on top of the pad and carpet.**

Install the tack strip the **thickness of your fingers away from the wall** or *3/8 of an inch*. This space is for the carpet to be tucked so it looks smooth around the walls. This space is called the **gully**. A carpet thinner than 3/8th of an inch will require less space to tuck than a thicker plush.

Remember to nail any ends of the tack strip that **don't have nails in them**, so that the strip is strong enough to stretch the carpet onto it. The tack strip is cut using a **tack strip cutter**, or you can also cut it using aviation snips.

When **installing pieces of tack strip in a doorway**, they are installed to follow the door jam, and allow room to tuck the carpet, but not over 3/8 of an inch of space. Two or three pieces must be used to keep the gully this correct distance. Pay attention to these small details for a quality job. Every piece of tack strip has a minimum of two nails, even very small pieces.

Sometimes there are **not any baseboards**

Lay the tack strip out around the room where it will be nailed. Face the pins towards the walls.

on the walls and *then, tack strip should be installed farther back* so that when the baseboard is put on, it's not on top of the tack strip. This would create a problem the next time carpet is installed. In this case, I install the strip, the thickness of the hammer head away from the wall. Test with a piece of the baseboard first.

When **installing up against hardwood floors** such as entry ways, the wood floor is usually 1/2 inch higher than the floor in the area to be carpeted. Install tack strip along the hardwood flooring as though it is a wall. As long as the hard wood floor is raised high enough to tuck the carpet next to, you can trim it with a wall trimmer and tuck it just like along a wall.

LEVELING FLOOR TRANSITIONS
If the floor that you are installing carpet next to, (tile, vinyl, or hardwood) is to high,

Quarter round is the half round wood strips that are placed around the baseboards. It is installed for wood floors and vinyl. For the best results, quarter round should be removed for carpet installation. Carpet may not stay tucked as well when installed with quarter round.

such as if the underlayment or durrock were too thick, then the carpet would be too low and the underlayment will show. You could also trip from the height difference.

The preferred levelers are rubber leveler strips, they come in various thicknesses, and in four foot lengths. They slope down gradually, are very durable and can not be felt under the floor. The other transition leveler used is wood shingles, they are nailed down, but do not come in long lengths.

Test for correct transition, if you are not sure about the height difference by using a piece of the carpet and tack strip next to the floor.

INSTALLING TACK STRIP ON A CONCRETE FLOOR

Some types of concrete are harder to nail than others. Concrete reaches its maximum strength after it has aged. When it is very hard you need to use a shorter thicker masonry nail. Fresh and very old concrete may be softer and a longer masonry nail can be used. There are other factors such as the type of mix used and how thinly the concrete was mixed that affects how well concrete will nail, but you simply need to experiment by test nailing.

Nailing the tack strip around the perimeter of the room. The pins face towards the wall to hold the carpet when stretching. Use the thickness of your fingers as a guide for how far away from the wall to place the tack strip.

To drive a concrete nail in, hit it square and on center with the hammer head. Re-nail any that don't drive in strongly with extra concrete nails or use a hammer drill.

DRILLING THE TACK STRIP

Sometimes the tack strip won't nail and hold firmly enough. Then it has to be drilled and nailed with **aluminum nails or flutted masonry nails**. This takes extra time but must be done, if there is any doubt that the strip is not secure. I recommend using a **Milwaukee hammer drill**.

Aluminum or masonry nails are nailed in to the drilled hole, this holds the tack strip very securely. For nailing into tack strip use 7/8th aluminum nails. Sometimes you only have to drill certain areas other times you will need to drill at every pre-nailed position in the tack strip.

Metals are always drilled and nailed with aluminum drives of flutted masonry nails on concrete. Metals are not as thick as the tack strip and uses a shorter, 5/8th inch aluminum nail.

There is a tool called a **T - Nailer,** that is used with an air compressor, to nail into concrete. I did not find it to save time personally, but some other installers like them.

Remember that it is fastest to tack strip the whole area to be carpeted completely in its entirety before moving on to installing padding.

Shown putting on knee pads. Always wear your knee pads to protect your knees, especially on the bare floor.

Use your fingers to position the tack strip the correct distance away from the wall. Approximatly 3/8th of an inch ,or less.

The assembly line method is the fastest method of working. Keep doing the same task until it is completed. In some cases where there is too much furniture, you can only work on one room at a time, because the other area is packed with furniture, this slows down the installation process.

INSTALLING METALS
Measure all doorways that need metals. They are used to finish off the edge next to **Vinyl Floors** and sometimes on wood floors to rooms not carpeted. Metals finish off entry ways, kitchens, and baths with vinyl. They are also used in basement doorways leading to utility rooms.

After accurately measuring the doorway, cut all the metals needed using Aviation Snips. Make sure that they're **not cut too wide** and scratch the wood work, but also **not too short** as

Install tackstrip next to a hard wood floor just as you would next to a wall. It is installed the same distance away from the hard wood as it is next to the wall.

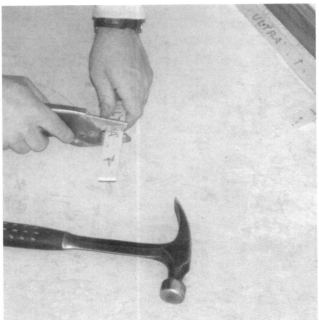

Cut the tack strip between the pins with strip cutters. Hold the piece of tack strip next to where it will be nailed to measure the correct size.

Installing the tack strip in the hallway.

to leave a space. **You will cut them very slightly shorter** (1/8th inch) than the doorway, and then divide any difference on each side.

If multiple layers of vinyl have been installed and now there is to thick of an underlayment, than a pin metal installed on top of the vinyl would leave a steep drop off, causing the carpet to float, like a trampoline when stretched. Shingles (sloped pieces of wood) or rubber leveler ramps should be used to ramp the transition. In very difficult transitions a flat bar metal may need to be used.

Metals are installed in the center of the door hinges, so that when the door is shut they can not be seen. Sometimes if a door is too low

Installing tack strip in the door jam; cut two or three pieces and angle them so that there is space to tuck the carpet. Install the strip 3/8th of an inch back, but not farther than this.

Pictured cutting the pin metal with aviation snips to fit to the width of doors. Measure each doorway accuratly before cutting. Nail the metals with ring shank nails on wood floors and 5/8th alumanum nails on concrete. Metals are used to finish off the carpet edge next to vinyl floors.

to close with the metal installed, you can keep it installed back farther so that the door does not have to be trimmed off. I use a **nail punch** to finish nailing down the nail, so that *the pins aren't smashed by the hammer head*. You don't want to smash too many pins in the metals or there won't be any to hold the carpet. A punch also drives in the nail to hold it more securely.

To make a square entry way with the metals; measure the area that you will place the metals. Then lay the metals in the place they will be installed, and mark them where you will cut. You then hammer down the metal lip in the area where you want them cut, so that you make an accurate cut. Use a miter box to cut the 45% angle so that they fit together. If you don't

Pictured is a room with tack strip installed properly along the walls. Tack strip is install 3/8th of an inch away from the walls.

hammer the lip down, where you will cut, the corner won't fit well. When it is hammered down with carpet installed, there will be a gap.

On a concrete floor the hammer drill and 5/8th aluminum nails are used. **Place nails on both ends** of the metal and then every one to two pre-made nail spaces apart. Pull on the metals, to make sure that they are installed solidly, they need to hold the stretch of the carpet.

TYPES OF METALS

There are different types of metals for different purposes. **Pin metals** are used for stretch in carpet, **pinless metals** are used for direct glue carpets, **stair nose** metals are used on the top edge of a step, **flat bar metals** are used to nail the metal directly over the top carpet edge. **Curved metals** can be used to curve corners for entry ways, instead of mitering square corners, or they also are used to make unique curved transitions between rooms not being carpeted.

Other transitions that can be used besides metals are, **wood moldings**, and **vinyl snap tracks**.

TURNING AND TACKING CARPET

Rolling an edge for transitions, instead of using metals, is called turning and tacking. Turning and tacking the edge of the carpet, refers

Pictured installing the metal in a doorway over a vinyl floor. Install the metals so that they are under the door. You do not want to be able to see the floor that is not being carpeted when the door is shut. I nail metals using ring shank nails and make sure that each end has been nailed and every other prestarted nail hole is nailed. It must hold solidly when power stretching the carpet. Use a nail punch to finish the nail so that you do not smash all of the pins down or hit the metal lip its self. The metal is supposed to look new!

METAL INSTALLATION DIAGRAMS

INCORRECT METAL POSITIONS

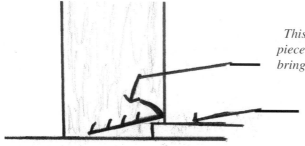

This metal is angled downward incorrectly; a piece of tack strip should be installed under it to bring the floor out further, so that the metal is level.

The Floor that is not to be carpeted is raised with underlayment and does not extend out into the room far enough so that the metal is level.

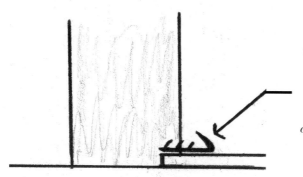

This metal is positioned incorrectly out into the room that is not being carpeted. It was positioned level, as it should be, but extends out past the door jam incorrectly. Install a piece of tackstrip in front of the underlayment and hammer down the pins to extend the underlayment farther out into the room to be carpeted.

to leaving the carpet edge long and rolling the edge underneath its self. You then staple with a **gilly gun** between the nap yarns. The type of carpet determines if turning and tacking is a good method to use.

Turning and tacking is not a recommended method with many carpets, but can be used with others. Stapling tends to show dimple marks, and creates a potential complaint. Some styles of carpet that have a denser, lower nap, will show flaws more, while higher, shaggier carpets, and many berbers won't show staples. Sculptured carpets that have an uneven nap level and multi color do not show staples as much as a level solid colored carpets.

Turning and tacking in a low visibility, low traffic area such as a closet door is permissible, but **caution should be used in deciding to turn and tack in high visibility situations.** Metals are often preferred over turning and tacking.

Staple every inch and **pull the nap yarns apart to staple in between the individual fibers**. This will prevent the nap from being stapled down. Make sure that you cut the edge to rolling under, so that it is not to long and hits the pad underneath. This will make a hump in the carpet. Leave the pad cut back an 1/1/2 inch to allow for turning under the carpet edge.

On the last riser of a step you also roll the carpet under, if the top landing is a wood or a tile floor.

CORRECT METAL POSITIONING

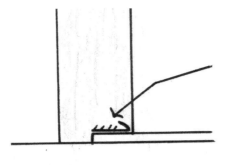

The metal is installed correctly within the door jam area. It is positioned level.

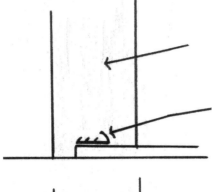

The door jam

Metal is installed correctly in the center of the door jam and is positioned level.

The metal is installed correctly within the door jam area.

The kitchen or bath room floor was not installed out far enough into the room to be carpeted.

Tack strip must be placed under the metal to ensure that it is level.

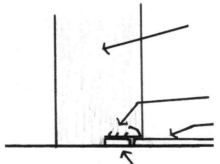

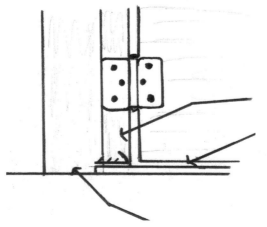

The Center of the door hinge with the metal positioned correctly under the door.

The metal finishes off the edge next to the vinyl flooring

The floor that is to be carpeted.

STEP EIGHT
INSTALLING PAD

Start preparing to install pad by loading your hammer stapler. The hammer stapler is used to staple padding to wood floors. *Have the staples out, and near by for quick refilling*. You don't want to have to run out of the room every time you need to reload the stapler.

Carry in all carpet padding being careful not to knock anything off the walls, that has not been removed. You may want to prop the front door open so it's easier to get in the house.

You lay all of the pad into position before beginning to staple. Roll out the carpet padding throughout the house and lay it into position. The pad comes in 6 foot wide rolls.

Lay the pad in a direction requiring the least amount of seams. Usually this is the same direction that the carpet will be running, but not always.

Staple the pad along the walls every 4-6 inches. The pad needs to be secured to the floor thoroughly enough so that when the carpet is being shifted into place and being stretched, it does not move.

The pad seams can be stapled, or duck taped, keep the staples a little closer than around the edges of the room. *Pad seams are stapled every two to three inches apart.* Pad seams are subject to pulling apart when the carpet is laid out so I advise duck taping them,

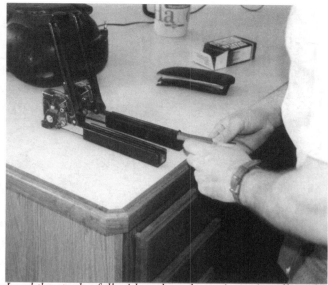
Load the stapler full with pad staples prior to installing the pad. Keep the staples near you while stapling because you will run out frequently.

they need to be very secure. **A pad seam that has pulled apart or rolled on top of its self will leave a hump under the carpet.** If you would miss fixing this and not notice until after the carpet was stretched in, you would have to pull all of the carpet back and fix the pad, then restretch the carpet.

If there is a possibility that a hard wood floor will be used in the future I would always tape the pad instead of stapling.

Using your carpet knife, **trim the pad next to the tack strip.** *Be careful not to leave any pad over lapping onto the tack strip, or to cut it to short leaving a gap.* Mistakes in cutting can be corrected with duck tape or if the pad should get

Roll the pad out through out the room and lay it into position. Pad is normally laid out in the same direction as the carpet unless you can run it in the opposite direction with less seams.

Stapling the pad along the walls. Space the staples 4 -6 inches apart along the walls. Staple close to the tackstrip but not on it.

Tape the pad seams with duck tape, or staple them with the hammer stapler. Seams are stapled with the staples spaced closer together than they are along the walls of the room. Staples are placed every 2 - 3 inches apart on seams.

Installing pad in the hallway.

torn when installing it, you simply tape it back together.

Make sure that **the staples are driven deeply enough so there is no chance of feeling them** through the carpet. The advantage of stapling the seams is that the pad is secured more tightly and won't shift out of place.

The advantage of taping is that there is no chance of feeling staples through the carpet and

Cutting the pad along the tack strip with a carpet knife. Cut next to the tack strip using it as a guide. Try not to leave any large gaps or to over lap on to the tack strip. You will not be able to hook the carpet onto the strip if the pad is on top of it.

a floor that may be used again won't have staples in it. I have stapled a lot of pad and never felt staples through the carpet. This is more likely to happen with a very cheap pad and carpet.

Seams are always taped together using duct tape on all concrete floors. This is obviously because you can not staple into a cement floor!

Top cut through both pieces of pad in doorways to make the pad seam. In the doorways you will have the pad from each room, flapped over each other. *With your carpet knife cut directly through both pieces.* Now you have a perfect seam to tape or staple together. When gluing pad on concrete *do not* tape the doorway seams until after the glue is poured. You will not be able to fold back the padding for gluing if the door seams are taped first.

Rebond pad dulls your knife blade more than the foam pads, *change knife blades frequently,* so it's easier to cut. When using a slotted blade (which has two sides for cutting) switch sides and use both sides of the bade. **Old time installers used sharpening stones to sharpen their knives.**

Hallways and closets have a lot of corners

Cutting through both layers of the pad for a doorway.

The pad fits together perfectly after top cutting through for a doorway.

and tend to take more time to trim than you would think, for their smaller size.

    Installing Pad Over The Top Riser. Wrap the pad over the top step and staple it above the tack strip. Trim the pad next to the tack strip, but not over lapping the tack strip. If the pad is on top of the tack strip you won't be able to stretch the carpet and have it hook on the pins.

    It's worth mentioning again that **it is fastest to complete each procedure in its entirety, rather than jumping to the next step,** before finishing. This is the factory **"assembly line theory"**. If you keep doing the same thing you don't lose your momentum. So if possible completely pad the entire house before moving on to the next step, " carrying in the carpet."

INSTALLING PAD ON CONCRETE

    Pad seams are always taped using duck tape on concrete floors. *Only tape the center pad seams and not the doorways* until after the pad is laid back into the glue. *You can't fold the pad back if the doorways are taped together.* The rest is glued along the outside edges of the floor.

    A glue specifically for gluing pad is used. Pad glue comes in *flammable* and *nonflammable* types, along with many different brands.

    Fold back the pad along all of the walls and pour the glue around the perimeter of the room. You can take a small piece of pad and use it to spread the glue out for better hold, or, I pour the glue in a zigzag pattern in and out on the floor for better hold.

    Once you have poured pad adhesive along the outside edges of the room floor you then lay

Staple the pad over the top step, then trim it above the tack strip.

the pad back into the glue.

You can walk along the edges to help press the pad into the glue so that it bonds firmly. Then finish taping the doorway seams.

Be careful not to get glue on your hands or walk in it. Its very sticky. Open some windows for ventilation and use nonflammable glue in closed areas next to furnaces or water heaters. There is also a type of pad adhesive that can be sprayed on from a can.

PAD SCRAPS

Pick up all pad scraps *being careful not to miss any small pieces because they will leave a bump under the carpet.*

Save the plastic bags that the pad comes in to reuse for picking up scraps, this will save your from purchasing as many garbage bags. I recommend recycling pad scraps and used clean pad that you have removed.

Rebond pad is laid out in a basement prior to being taped and glued.

Pad seams are taped with duct tape on concrete floors.

Pictured picking up pad scraps. Pad is recycled; so keep the pad separated from carpet and other waste.

Pad adhesive is poured around the perimeter of the room for concrete pad installation.

QUIZ
SECTION TWO
Part One

1. Doors that open _____ need to be taken off?
    (a) Into the bathroom.
    (b) Into the attic.
    (c) Into the area that is being carpeted.
    (d) None of the doors should be removed.

2. When taking off doors you should?
    (a) Not worry about where you put them.
    (b) Organize them in a way so that you know which door goes where.
    (c) Number the door hinges with a pencil.
    (d) Both b and c.

3. Some ways of marking a door so that you know where it went are.......
    (a) Write a number on the hinges with marker.
    (b) Systematically arrange the door pins differently in each door.
    (c) Scratching it with a nail.
    (d) don't take off the doors.

4. To carry a door properly you...
    (a) grip it firmly in both hands and tilt the top downward.
    (b) watch very carefully that you do not bang the door corner into any walls or ceilings.
    (c) carry it with the top tilted slightly sideways.
    d) all of the above.

5. To remove a door you....
    (a) remove the pins from the hinges.
    (b) use a nail and a hammer.
    (c) unscrew the door hinges.
    (d) both a and b.

Answers
1. c 2. d 3. b 4. d 5. d

QUIZ
SECTION TWO
Part Two

1. Tack strip is installed how far away from the baseboard?
    (a) 2 inches.
    (b) 3/8 of an inch.
    (c) The thickness of your fingers.
    (d) Both b & c.

2. Tack strip for concrete has?
    (a) Concrete nail.
    (b) Shorter Nails than wood strip.
    (c) Long Narrow Nails.
    (d) Both a & b.

3. Metals are installed?
    (a) As far into the other room as possible.
    (b) Any place you want them.
    (c) Under the door hinges.
    (d) We don't use any metals.

4. When there are not any nails on the ends of a piece of tack strip?
    (a) Put an extra nail.
    (b) Don't worry about it.
    (c) Ask the customer what to do.
    (d) Tell your partner to do it.

5. A metal that is installed incorrectly is.......
    (a) positioned into the room that is not being carpeted.
    b) has nails in each end and every four inches.
    (c) positioned in the center of the door hinges.
    (d) positioned so that it is level.

Answers
1. d 2. d 3. c 4. a 5. a

MULTIPLE CHOICE QUIZ
SECTION TWO
Part Three

1. You attach pad to a wood floor using?
  (a) A hammer stapler.
  (b) Carpet glue.
  (c) Chewing gum.
  (d) Carpet glue.
  (e) Power stretcher.

2. Pad seams are attached using?
  (a) Duck tape.
  (b) A Hammer stapler.
  (c) Pad glue.
  (d) Both a & 3.

3. When trimming pad.....
  (a) Don't worry if it's over the tack strip.
  (b) Don't worry if you trim it 3 inches away from the tact strip.
  (c) Trim it next to the tack strip without cutting it to short or leaving it to long.
  (d) Use a dull knife blade.
  (e) trim it next to the wall.

4. You install pad on a concrete floor using....
  (a) a hammer stapler.
  (b) duck tape.
  (c) pad adhesive.
  (d) both b and c.

5. Be careful to pick up all small pieces of pad as....
  (a) they are valuable and must be recycled.
  (b) it will kill time before lunch.
  (c) the carpet will not be stretched tightly.
  (d) it will leave a bump under the carpet.

Answers
1. a
2. d
3. c
4. d
5. d

MULTIPLE CHOICE QUIZ
SECTION TWO
Part Four

1. When you carry in your tools you should set them?
  (a) In the middle of the room.
  (b) Some place out of the way so you don't have to keep moving them.
  (c) In the basement.
  (d) Both a and c.

2. When you get to the job you should?
  (a) Eat your lunch.
  (b) Stretch in the carpet.
  (c) Carry in the tools needed.
  (d) Carry in the hammer drill.

3. When rolling up the carpet you?
  (a) Mark any corner you want.
  (b) Roll it all up the same direction.
  (c) Don't have to worry about rolling it up straight.
  (d) Mark the same corner on each roll.
  (e) Both b & d.

4. Always roll the cut pieces of carpet up ....
  (a) sideways.
  (b) opposite directions.
  (c) the same direction.
  (d) all of the above.

5. List three methods that you use to ensure that the carpet is all running the same direction....
1.
2.
3.

Answer
1. b
2. c
3. e
4. c
5. 1. Rolling all cuts up the same direction. 2. Marking the same corner an each cut. 3. Checking the nap direction in the house.

STEP 9
CARRYING IN CARPET

Carrying in a heavy roll of carpet requires some assistance.

Carrying in carpet is sometimes impossible to do alone. Although it can be done by yourself, there are times when you can not carry in a heavy roll of carpet without some help. There are some situations such as **getting a large heavy roll of carpet around a corner**, or carrying carpet up and down stairs that make it an impossible task to carry alone.

There are techniques to carrying in carpet with a partner. Coordinate with your partner which shoulder you are carrying the carpet on so that you both have the roll on the same shoulder. Walk at a steady pace at the same speed as your partner. Don't push by walking out of sync with him. Do not drop the carpet unexpectedly, give a warning to your partner. Once you are ready to let the carpet down, do so on the count of three, under as much control as possible.

It's a good idea to **prop open the front door** so that you do not struggle to get the carpet through.

If there are pictures and breakables on

Prop open the front door of the house when carrying in carpet.

A two wheel dolly will make carrying in even a heavy roll of carpet by your self much easier.

the walls, be careful not to knock anything off. **Remove anything from the walls** that may be knocked off.

The backing of many types of carpet are very coarse, like sandpaper, so, **be very careful of rubbing it against woodwork,** and the corners of the walls when carrying in the carpet. Carpet is easier to handle when its bent and tied with a binge cord, especially if you are working alone.

It can be a struggle getting a 12 foot roll of carpet around corners. **The carpet often has to be bent to get around corners.** In a difficult area such as a basement you can check to see if there are any windows that the carpet could be brought through.

Carrying in a heavy roll of carpet by yourself can be back breaking work. Using a bungie cord to tie the carpet in half makes it easier to carry in by yourself. The shorter length helps you to go around corners without such a struggle. Using a two wheel dolly can make it possible to carry in a very heavy carpet alone, if you are able to bend and tie the carpet to a shorter length.

Different types of carpets vary greatly in their weights depending on the thickness of the nap and the type of backing. Of course a fifteen foot wide carpet is going to be heavier than a twelve foot wide.

STEP 10
LAYING OUT THE CARPET

Laying out the carpet isn't as easy as you would think. **You can't always roll it straight across the room unless the room is wider than the roll of carpet** and then a seam will be required.

The roll of carpet can be positioned catty cornered in a room that's smaller than the roll and pulled out as pictured. Grip the opened flap of carpet and pull straight up over your head, unrolling the carpet. This will not have unrolled all of the carpet. Next, back spin the remaining amount out on top of its self. Neatly fold the sides in so that you have the carpet folded in a

square near the center of the room. Once the carpet is folded then it's easy to turn it to the proper direction. Next, unfold the carpet into place. This is one of the secrets to laying out carpet in a room that is too small to roll the carpet out in.

In a room that is 11 x 35 **the carpet is rolled out in opposite direction of the room that it will actually go.** You then turn it to run the proper direction. This is the opposite direction that you intend for the carpet to run when you are finished. The roll of carpet is 12 foot wide and the room is 11 foot wide so you roll it out with the 12 foot carpet going in the 35 foot direction of the room, across the room. Then you fold the carpet and turning it into place. It's impossible to lay out most rooms with out using this trick.

All of the carpet of the same type runs the same direction in the house, unless they are not directly connected to each other or completely different types of carpet.

When you cut the carpet you rolled every piece up the same direction, so that if you roll out each piece in the house, **the same way,** they all will be going the **same direction.**

The size of each roll was written on the **same corner** of each piece, so the **same corner in each room** of the house will have the size written on it.

There are some **other methods of checking the nap direction.** You can check the nap direction by **running your hand across the carpet nap.** Some carpets are difficult to determine the nap direction when using this method and you can be fooled. And in some cases the carpet can have a reverse nap, tricking you in to thinking that they're going the same direction when they are not.

Most carpets have arrows marked on the backing from the factory, and these arrows don't lie, where as nap direction sometimes can. Even if there are not arrows on the backing, there are often lines marking down the backing that will be on the same side of all pieces of carpet.

Another trick to show nap direction is to lay a piece of writing paper on the carpet nap, and

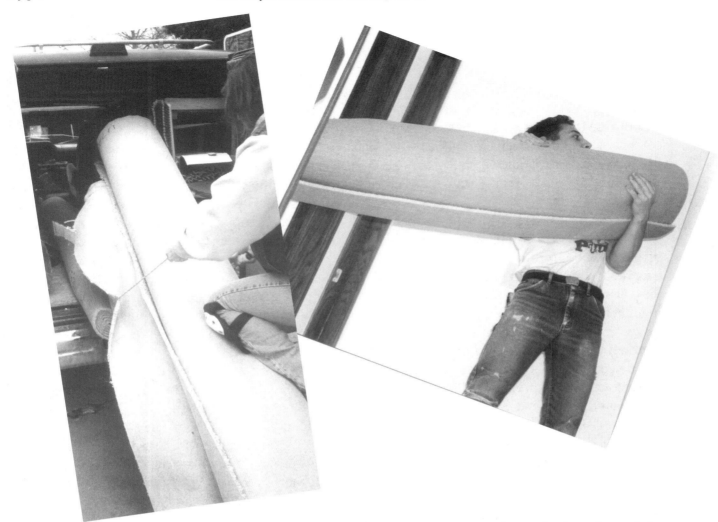

When working by yourself, you can bend the roll in half outside and tie a binge cord around it, so that it can be carried around corners inside the house. When carrying in around corners, be careful not to scuff the wood work. It's easier to carry in with a partner, and bend the carpet to get it around corners.

with a smooth seam tractor roll on the paper, it will move the paper in the direction that the nap is laying. It does not matter which way you roll on the piece of paper, it will move it in the direction the nap is laying.

A final method of **determining that a piece of carpet is not quarter turned** (turned sideways) is by examining the nylon threads in the backing, the length threads (warp threads) are of a different type than the width threads (weft threads).

Always use multiple methods for carpet direction and you will ensure that mistakes are never made. The nap must all go the same direction or the carpets will look different colors.

When would you not have to run all of the carpet the same direction? If the rooms were **complexly separated,** such as by a vinyl entry way. If the carpets being installed are of **different types,** such as the hallway being a different type or color than the bed rooms. Also this would be beneficial if one area laid out with less seams or less yardage by turning it. but only when the areas are separated or if different carpets are used.

The carpet needs to be positioned so that just the right amount is up the walls, at least two inches, and so that it falls through all doorways. Make sure that its centered squarely and not short on any walls or corners.

You can shift a piece of carpet into position by side-kicking it with the side of you foot to fine tune its positioning. Be careful that you don't kick with your heel as it is possible to kick a hole in the carpet. Most mistakes can be repaired but why make an avoidable mistake. Also make sure that your shoes are not dirty when you side kick the carpet.

The other method of shifting the carpet is to pull it. Pulling a carpet up the wall is very difficult if its laid out in a long room, as you are pulling one side the center of the carpet buckles and wrinkles. It is most effective to pull the carpet when the length is folded back on to itself then it doesn't bind on the pad and buckle. These are important tricks you will want to remember when you try to lay out the carpet. Make sure

that no one is standing on the carpet when you try to pull it. That will make it just a little bit heavier.

Once you are **sure** that it is laid *where you want it*, you can make some rough cuts so that there isn't a large excess up the walls. This makes it easier to work with when stretching and trimming. Some corners need to have relief cuts made so the carpet will lay into place. Relief cuts can be made leaving an inch extra and still let the carpet fold down into an area.

Never cut a piece of carpet until you are sure that it is in the proper position. A common situation is for an installer to cut the carpet into an entry way metal and when he finished he realized that the carpet was still six inches away from the opposing wall doorway, and needed to

The excess carpet is cut off so that several inches are up each wall.

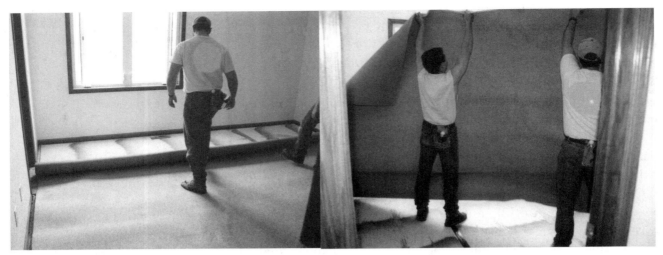

One technique for rolling out carpet in a room that is to narrow is to place it catty corner in the room and pull the open end straight up over your head.

Rolling the carpet roll straight out across the room is possible if the room is wide enough.

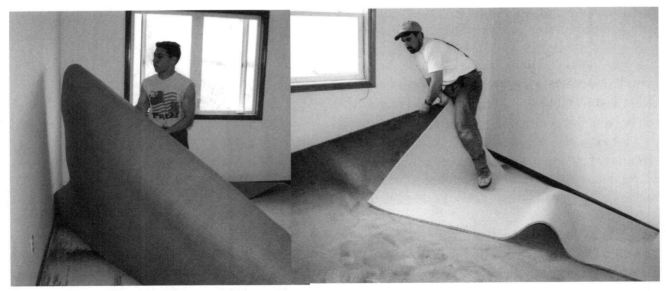

Once the roll of carpet is unrolled it can be unfolded in the room.

Side kicking is a method of shifting the carpet straight in the room.

be pulled in the opposite direction. You would wind up being at least six inches short of the metal and have to seam it. This is a very important rule so I will repeat it. **Never cut** a piece of carpet until you are sure that its in the proper position.

You trim off the excess carpet so that 2-3 inches remain up the walls. Its better to leave extra than to be short on carpet. Make sure that the carpet lays through door ways with enough extra. Make sure it goes over top steps. Walk around the perimeter of the room checking that every wall , corner and doorway has adequate carpet before making any cuts.

Relief cuts are the cuts you make to allow the carpet to be laid around corners.

Many of the relief cuts are not made until after stretches are made, because you can stretch past corners. You can usually stretch the carpet first, and then make the corner cuts so that it will lay into areas such as closets.

It's OK to make a cut if you know you will be stretching in that direction, and will gain carpet. If you are stretching away from a corner you could wind up short on carpet with an inch cut showing.

Stretching past a corner is not that big of a deal, and can be repaired with a glue gun. Its a somewhat common occurrence and once repaired not noticeable, **but** it is preventable so take precautions.

SCUFFING WOOD WORK AND PAINT

Scuffing off paint, on corners and scuffing wood work are often an inevitable part of laying out, and installing carpet. Contractors know this and touch up the paint after installation. I wipe off the woodwork when finished with the installation. Let the customer know that you are being as cautious as possible, but there may still be scuffs. The customer may need to touch up the paint after installation.

Be very careful of woodwork when laying out the carpet. Don't just drop carpet into place or force it roughly around corners. Treat each home as if it is your own. Laying out the carpet can scuff paint off of baseboards, wall corners and walls. The backing is rough like a piece of sand paper.

A soft back carpet is manufactured with a soft felt attached to the backing of the carpet. It will prevent scuffs.

Cardboard can be taped on to wall corners to protect them, when laying out the carpet.

Woodwork on baseboards that are scuffed up after installing carpet, is not scratched deeply just roughly sanded. Polyurethane on the woodwork shows white scuffs when sanded.

Scuff marks on wood work can be wiped off with old English wood oil and magically disappear. Old English comes in light through dark colors to match the wood work color.

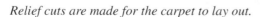

Relief cuts are made for the carpet to lay out.

QUIZ -
Carrying in & laying out the carpet

1. When carrying in a heavy roll of carpet you should?
    (a) Hurry as fast as you can so you don't strain yourself.
    (b) Bring a forklift with you.
    (c) Take it easy going through the house and be careful not to rub against walls or break anything.
    (d) Drop it as soon as you get inside.

2. When you are carrying carpet around corners you should?
    (a) Bend the carpet so that it will go around easy.
    (b) Cut the roll in half using your knife.
    (c) Not worry about rubbing against the walls or hitting someone with it.
    (d) Use a two wheeler.

3. When you carry in a roll of carpet by yourself you can?
    (a) Drag it through dirt and mud.
    (b) Bend it in half and tie it with a binge. cord so that its easier to get around corners.
    (c) Go home early.
    (d) Schedule an appointment with the chiropractor.

4. When carrying in a roll of carpet with a partner....
    (a) do not push by walking out of sync with him.
    (b) carry the carpet on the same shoulder.
    (c) do not drop the carpet unexpectedly.
    (d) all of the above.

5. Its a good idea to prop the front door of the house open when carrying in so that.....
    (a) you air out the house.
    (b) the pets can come and go as they wish.
    (c) its not a struggle to open the door while carrying a roll of carpet.
    (d) both b and c.

6. When laying out the carpet?
    (a) Cut it down to the smallest size possible.
    (b) Make sure its in the proper position before making any cuts.
    (c) Allow an extra 14 inches up each wall.
    (d) stand on top of it as you're trying to shift it.

7. You can shift a piece of carpet into position by?
    (a) Kicking with the side of your foot.
    (b) Pulling with your hands.
    (c) Both A & B.
    (d) none of the above.

Answers
1. c 2. a 3. b 4. d 5. c 6. b 7. c

STEP 11
SEAMING CARPET

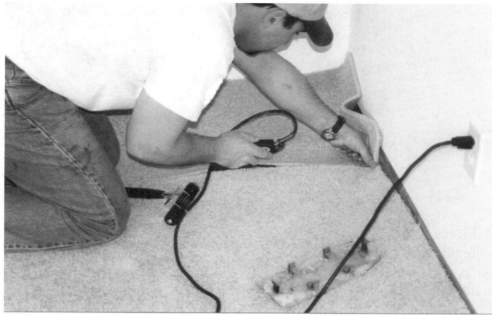
Pictured starting a seam

Many times the room is wider than the width of the carpet, and will require a seam.

Today most seams are make using a **hot melt seam tape** and a **seaming iron**.

In the past all seams were hand sewn with a **needle** and **thread,** today only certain carpets and specialty applications are hand sewn.

Seaming is a very important part of how the finish carpet job looks. Seaming is a learned skill that is perfected with practice.

No one wants seams in their home that stand out like a sore thumb. Not all types of carpets seam up as invisibly as others, and not all lay out positions hide seams well.

Some carpets show seams more than others, for example, a carpet with a short dense pile and light color, would show a seam more than one with a higher uneven type pile and with multi-colors.

CUTTING THE CARPET EDGE

First the edge of the carpet needs to be cut off to make a good seam. This is because the edge of the carpet is not straight, and it becomes frayed with the nap (pile) loose and falling out from the transporting of the carpet. Seams will not look good with damaged carpet edges.

Once the carpet is laid in position to seam, **one inch is cut off** with a **row cutter** or **straight edge**. A row cutter is always used on berbers and level loop carpets.

In the past all plush carpets were cut using a straight edge, now it's known that plush carpets have rows just as berbers and level loop carpets do, and can be row cut.

Be careful of the edge once it has been cut. Don't walk on freshly cut edges ready to be seamed.

Once you start running the seamer down the seam, you don't want to be interrupted, its best not to stop in the middle of a seam.

Pictured row cutting one inch off of the plush carpet to prepare it to be seamed.

ROW CUTTING

It is very important to row cut **berber type carpets**, unlike plush carpets, the nap (pile) will fray out when they are cut through.

Some carpets don't have straight rows and must to be straight edged. Try row cutting first; you will be able to see if the rows are straight. Row cutting is the preferred method because you don't cut through any of the nap (pile) as when straight edging.

The **row cutter** is for cutting the edge off while the **row runner** is a tool used to spread open the row, and make following the row easier.

To use a row cutter you must first **spread the rows apart** and **create a line** down the row.

Straight edging plush carpet is still a good method. Straight edging often gives you a straighter edge than row cutting and then will give you a better looking seam. Use a tape measure to ensure a even cut. Don't cut too deep, only cut through the backing or the pile on the carpet will be cut.

This is done by running a **row runner** down the row. You can follow the line make by row running.

Row running also opens the rows apart so they cut without cutting any nap. There is a tool sold specifically for spreading open the rows, but many installers use a straight screw driver or a comb as a row runner. The cheap black combs work very well as a row runner. I find they work very well with berber carpets. A flat head screw driver seems to work best for me with plush carpets. I find that a larger screw driver works better (without snagging) than a smaller one. This works as a guide to follow behind with the row cutter.

MAKING IT WORK OR SENDING IT BACK ?

Making a defective carpet work is not always the answer if it will not look satisfactory when seamed. But a good installer can often do a lot to make a defective product work. The biggest problems are: excessively crooked rows, pattern bowed, pattern out of skew, and pattern elongation.

What do you do when you come against a berber that you can not get the row runner to go down any row? It seems to snag. **This method can work in a difficult case:** Some carpets are cross stitched and you won't be able to run a screw driver or comb through the rows. In this

Seaming the length seam of the room. This seam is half finished.

case you can pull a yarn out and it will make a row all the way down the carpet that you can run the row cutter down. This is a handy trick to use. You can work with difficult carpets if you develop the skill level. I wouldn't send back a carpet with cross stitched rows, this is not necessarily a defective carpet.

CROOKED ROWS - If a plush carpet does not run a straight row, I recommend straight edging it. Plush carpets do not need to be row cut, and a straight edge will give you a very straight cut.

Berber and level loop carpets need to be row cut. If the rows are excessively crooked and you can not get the backings together, then you either must send back the carpet or make it work. If a berber carpet has excessively crooked rows, I recommend trying to row cut extra rows in the areas that seem to veer out unevenly.

Berber or level loop carpet with very

crooked rows may need to be sent back rather than make an installation that no one is going to be happy with.

PATTERN BOWED - The pattern bow is in the 12 foot width of the carpet. If a pattern is bowed more than 1 inch over 12 foot than it is defective. Use a chalk line to check the pattern bow.

PATTERN OUT OF SKEW - The skew is the pattern in the length of the carpet. If it is out of skew more than 1 inch over a 12 foot length than the carpet is defective. Use a chalk line to check the pattern skew.

PATTERN ELONGATION - In this situation the pattern starts by matching but elongates as it progresses. The pattern will not match. The seam can some times be stretched to make this pattern match.

COLOR DYE VARIATION - The color through out the carpet must be exactly the same or the color in the seam will look completely different. There is not much you can do to fix this but to send the carpet back.

STRAIGHT EDGING CARPET

Straight edging a plush carpet is still a viable method of trimming off the edge to be seamed. Although row cutting does not cut through any nap, it also does not usually make as straight of a cut as a straight edged cut does.

You may find plush, commercial, and

Seaming carpet using a tractor to press the carpet into the adhesive. A wood board is used as a seam weight.

kitchen carpets that will not row cut straight enough to seam, and have the backing fit evenly together. Some carpets cannot be row cut with out much unnecessary difficulty.

To straight edge a seam you cut from the back of the carpet. You can not fold the carpet straight back and start the cut, because it would be up the wall, and impossible to start.

You must fold back the carpet one side at a time. I straight edge as far as I can, then fold back from the other side to finish cutting.

Use a 6 foot straight edge and measure one inch in from the edge of the carpet, top and bottom.

Always **use a new knife blade** when cutting seams. Do not cut to deeply or you will cut the nap and create shorties (nap that is cut through).

Place your knee on the straight edge and hold the top securely so that it doesn't move. Cut down as far as you can without moving your knee.

Slide the straight edge down, **use the top cut in the carpet as a guide for the top measurement**. Measure in one inch on the bottom carpet edge, using the tape measure align the straight edge.

Some installers think they can move the

straight edge down with out measuring, by running the straight edge along the first cut. You would think that you could line up the straight edge with the first cut and continue running straight, but this doesn't work. You always run off crooked.

LATEXING THE CARPET EDGE

Cut carpet edges are applied with a bead of latex. A white liquid, the consistency of Elmer glue, that is applied with an applicator bottle. This bonds in the nap (pile) yarns to keep the yarns from fraying out with wear.

A very small amount is applied to the carpet backing, right along the cut edge without getting any in the nap (pile) itself.

You do not want to apply too much latex or get any in the nap or it will work itself up into the nap and create a poor looking seam. Latex is a glue like substance that keeps the nap (pile) yarns from falling out and unraveling in the seams.

Carpet backing is latexed from the factory and it is controversial as to whether it's the installers responsibility to apply extra latex. With seam welding latexing becomes unnecessary.

If a seam is fraying out and the carpet mill comes to look at it they will use a black light to determine if latex was applied. If it was not and you did not seam weld the carpet, then you may be responsible for the carpet fraying even though a cheaply constructed carpet itself could be the cause of the problem.

Seam welding can be accomplished by either applying a thermal seam seal or by using a specialized seam welding iron

THERMAL SEAM SEAL

Another method of sealing the cut seam edges is to use a hot melt glue gun. Apply a bead of glue to the cut edge, and then leave it dry. Then seam the carpet with hot melt seam tape as usual.

The carpet edges to be seamed are sealed with Latex as shown. This step can be avoided by using a seam welding iron for seaming. This iron applies thermal glue to the cut edges while hot melt seaming. Seaming with this iron accomplishes two tasks at once and creates a very strong seam.

The thermal glue will melt and bond the backings together, sealing the edge. This is called seam welding.

This method welds the backing together, preventing seam peaking. If the carpet is bent the seam will not open up as is the case with using only traditional hot melt seaming tape. It also welds the pile yarns back together preventing the pile from fraying.

The best method of seam welding is to use a seam weld iron made by Taylor Tools. It applies adhesive to the cut edges while you are hot melt seaming. These seams will not fray, as the pile yarns are welded together. Seams will not open up when bent and will not peak when stretched.

SEAM TAPE

Seam tape is covered with **glue beads** that are melted with the hot seam iron to glue the carpet together.

Seam tape comes in various types, widths, qualities, and brands.

Crain and **Roberts** are two main brands.

They come in different qualities, usually described as the rows of glue beads on the tape. An 11 row seam tape is top quality.

The most common seam tape width is 3 inches and that is the width of a standard seam iron. There is a 6 inch tape that requires a 6 inch iron. The theory is that it prevents seam peaking (an upward peak in the seam area that can occur after the carpet is stretched).

The seam tape is positioned under the area to be seamed. Make sure that it is positioned with equal portions for each piece of carpet.

The ends of the seams are the most difficult areas to bond properly. Allow several inches to run up the walls. You can fold the extra seam tape over the back of the iron and melt it to secure the seam up the wall. Pull up on the front of the iron to melt the first several inches of seam tape.

POSITIONING THE CARPET

The carpet pieces must all fit perfectly

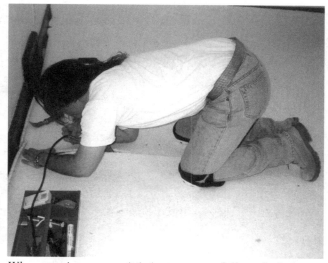

When starting a seam it is important to fully melt the seam tape on the tack strip. This is a problem area. The seam tape can be folded over the iron to melt the tape up the wall.

together before beginning the seam. Make sure that it is not over lapped, or has any gaps in the seam area. Gaps can be forced together somewhat when seaming, so that the edge fits flush together.

RUNNING THE SEAM

The **seam iron** is used to melt the glue on the seam tape. A 3 inch iron is all you need, I don't think the 6 inch irons are necessary. Spend your money on a good 3 inch iron and good seam tape.

Allow your seam iron to heat up adequately before beginning the seam. The iron has numbers that give reference to its temperature and can be adjusted. Refer to the owners manual and the recommendations of the seam tape you are using to determine the setting.

Start with a lower temperature and determine if you need to increase the temperature by how well the glue is melting on the tape.

Keep the iron out of the way of traffic so that no one knocks it over while it is warming up. Use a scrap of pad or carpet to set it on, in case it is knocked over.

Start the seam by straddling the seam area so you can look directly into the seam area, and make sure that the backings are butt evenly together.

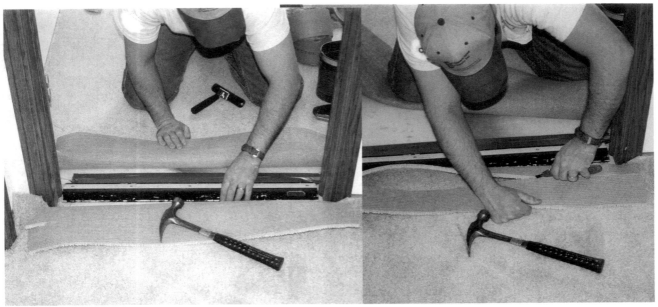

A doorway seam being cut using a seam mate.

The seam mate makes a cut in the backing, then you finish the cut with a knife.

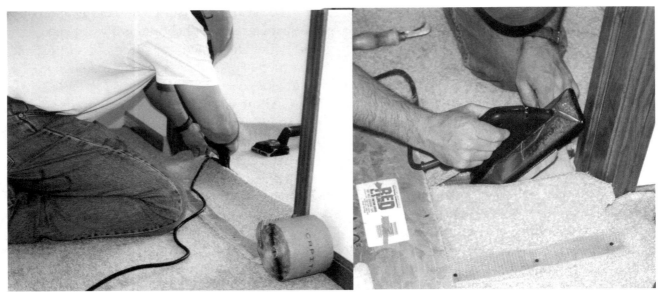

seaming a doorway.

Pulling the iron out at the end of a doorway seam can be tricky. Pull it straight up and out being careful not to get glue on the door jam.

Use your hands and legs to move the carpet if it's not perfectly together.

Start at one end of the room to begin the seam, fold one corner over so that it's easier to place the iron under the carpet.

Remove the iron from its tray and slide the tray to the other end of the seam so you have it when you're finished.

Place the iron on top of the seam tape and push it right against the wall, on top of the tack strip. It is difficult to achieve a thorough bond at the ends so a trick that I use is to fold the extra seam tape running up the wall over the top of the iron to melt more glue. It takes roughly one minute for the glue to melt adequately. But don't go by time, go by if the glue is melted thoroughly.

Move the iron forward slightly and check that the glue is melted properly. It will appear slightly golden brown but not burnt. For a strong seam bond you must have the glue fully melted, but not left on any longer than this. Each time the glue is melted move the iron forward the full length of the iron. Do not go past the area where the glue is not melted. You would leave a space without the carpet seamed at all.

Pressing the carpet into the glue quickly, you don't want it to start drying. Use your hands and legs to push the carpet closer together or farther apart so that the backing is evenly together with no spaces or over laps.

You then **use a tractor to press the carpet into the glue**. Do not press excessively hard or glue could be pushed up through the seam.

SEAM WEIGHT

Use a seam weight to hold pressure on the seam. For years I used my tool box tray, with wood underlayment on the bottom of the tray, to press the carpet into the glue. I switched to a solid wood piece of oak for a seam weight to help the seam cool more efficiently.

Pull the seam weight behind the seam iron. You don't need a heavy weight pressing down, but enough to press the carpet into the glue and hold it down. Too heavy of a weight could force the glue up through the seam.

A steel weight could draw heat and adhesive up through the seam. If a tool box tray is used a piece of wood should be glued onto the bottom of the tray. I recommend you use a solid wood seam weight.

You finish the end of the seam to the side of the seam, because the wall will be in your way.

Never walk on or near seams being made until the glue is dry and the seam cool. It takes about 15-20 minutes for a seam to cool.

SEAMING ON BOARDS

Seam boards are thin pieces of underlayment cut 1 foot wide by various lengths from 3-6 feet. They are used to give a firm seaming surface and to keep the seam tape from sticking to the padding.

Seam boards are placed on top of the pad and under the seam area. If you are using a foam pad, this gives a firm surface to seam on, the soft pad is to spongy to give a firm seaming surface.

It isn't as necessary to use seam boards on a rebond pad as this pad is firm enough, but the seam tape may still stick to the pad.

The board is slid to keep it under the iron by pulling it with you under the seam. Some installers cut a handle or use a rope to pull the board along.

After the seam is cool fold back the carpet to get the board out. Do not use seam boards in areas that you can not fold the carpet back (doorways) to get the board out unless you have a string attached to the seam board so it can be pulled out.

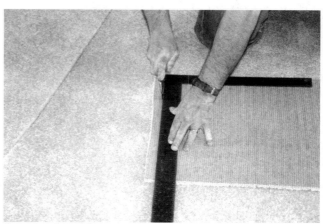

A square is used to cut cross seams.

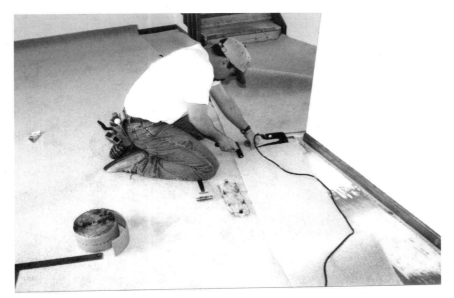

The cross seam is being seamed together

CROSS SEAMS

Seams are often not done in one long piece because of the necessity of having all of the carpet going in the same direction. When installing one room versus three, the piece of carpet ordered for one seam is too short to do it in one piece. You may have to do it in three or four pieces for one room.

Cross seams are the shorter seams in the long seam. Cross seams are usually avoided on larger jobs because there are more seams and a larger piece of carpet is ordered for all of them. Ordering extra carpet can often cut down on cross seams.

A square is used to cut cross seams. Sometimes they can also be row cut to achieve a better looking seam.

Rows do not always run both length ways and cross ways in all carpets, and when they do they usually are not square with each other. The square is usually most effective in this case.

Some installers seam the cross seams first, but I prefer to seam them last after I have completed the length seam. Just be careful that everything is fit together perfectly.

DOORWAY SEAMS

Doorway seams are the most difficult seam to make. It can be tricky to cut them to fit per-

fectly together. They tend to either bow from being cut too long or are cut too short and have a gap. With a little practice you will find that doorway seams are not that difficult to cut.

Doorway seams are cut in several ways, with a tool called a seammate, or with a straight edge or square.

You have two flaps of carpet that need to be cut to make a doorway seam. One from each room. A seammate is a tool that is placed in the center of the door hinged and has a razor blade running the length of it. Lay one of the doorway pieces of carpet over the seammate; use a plastic seam tractor and roll on top of the carpet to make the cut. It won't cut all of the way through, but will leave a good cut mark down the carpet backing. You finish cutting by folding back the carpet, then you use your knife with a sharp blade to finish the cut.

Now position the seammate so that there is a 1/8th inch space from the edge that was just cut. If you would cut the other piece to fit exactly with the first one just cut it would be to long and they would bow. Now fold the piece just cut out of the way and lay the other flap of carpet over the blade. Be very careful that the seammate does not move out of place. Now use the seam tractor to roll on the carpet over the blade. Thoroughly roll up and down the blade to cut the carpet.

Be very careful that the seammate doesn't

Remove the seam tape from old carpet. You can heat up the tape from the back using the seam iron, then remove the old seam tape.

move when rolling on it.

Seammates come in 23 inch and 29 inches wide to fit various doorways. They don't fit perfectly, but are slid to finish the seam. I mark the pad with a marker along the seammate so I know that the seam mate hasn't move when rolling to cut. The mark on the pad is used to guide you when sliding the seammate over to finish the last part of the cut.

Doorway seams can also be cut using a square or straight edge.

Cut a small cut in the carpet on both sides of the door jam. Next, fold back the carpet and place the straight edge across the marks you just made in the carpet. Now lay this cut side over the other side that is to be cut. You now make two small cuts through the top being guided by the edge of the carpet just cut. Leave a 1/8th inch space because the carpets when cut too long without leaving this space will then bow, as they are too long.

Row cutting both sides for a doorway seam is not usually effective. The rows won't run straight in both rooms and the seam often won't line up.

REMOVING THE IRON ON DOOR SEAMS

Fold one corner of the carpet back, and slide the iron out sideways. Then set the iron back into the tray. This method avoids getting any glue on the woodwork. Keep the iron on a scrap of carpet, away from traffic.

Some installers prefer to pull the iron straight up the door jam. I prefer the first method.

SEAM WELDING

The cut backing of the carpet to seam is bonded back together using a thermal adhesive. This is done with a hot melt seam gun or a seam welding iron. Seam welding prevents seam fraying and seam peaking.

When seaming with a traditional seam tape and iron, only the backings of the carpet are seamed. When you bend this carpet the seam will open and you will see that the nap yarns are not glued. With seam welding the carpet seams do not open up in the splice as much and you will weld the nap yarns back together creating a superior seam.

Thermal glue can be used as a seam seal. It is applied with a glue gun. Apply it to the cut edges first, then allow it to dry. You can then seam the carpet with hot melt seam tape and the thermal glue will re-melt, bonding the cut backings and welding the nap yarns and backing together.

The best method of seam welding that I know of is to use a specialized seam iron, the seam welding iron. This iron allows you to seam weld and hot melt seam simultaneously.

Taylor Tools manufactures a seam welding iron. They offer a seam welding hands-on training course to learn to use this iron.

TAYLOR TOOLS
Web: www.taylortools.com

SEAMING ONTO OLD CARPET

Seaming onto old carpet is often done when installing a hallway and seaming the doorways to bed rooms that will not have the carpet replaced. The old seam tape will still be stuck onto the back of the carpet you want to seam onto.

You fold over the carpet and set the seam iron on the back of the old seam tape to melt it, so that it pulls off easily. You can try pulling it off but often this will only tear the carpet edge.

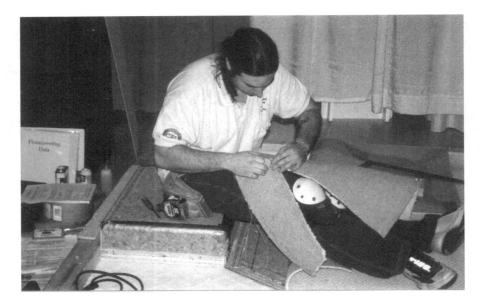

Pictured hand sewing a step that is two different colors. One color on the front of the step, and one on the rest of the step. The carpet must be wrapped over the step in one piece.

PATTERN MATCHING

There are many types of patterns in carpet, some are obvious, and easy to match, others must be studied.

Patterns must be matched in the width (side matching) and in the length. Most berbers that you are seaming edge to edge only need the first inch cut off, and are manufactured to fit without any side shifting. Usually you will need to cut into the width for side matching also.

Patterned carpet will require extra carpet, this amount varies depending on the pattern, some matching can require up to 4 feet of extra carpet.

Some kitchen carpets have small diamond patterns and can not be row cut. To cut the carpet and cut in the center of the diamonds you have to cut from the top with a straight edge.

Either fold back the carpet below to top cut or lay underlayment on the floor under where you will be cutting. Line up the 6 foot straight edge lined up down the center of the diamonds.

TYPES OF PATTERN MATCHES

SET PATTERN MATCH - The pattern units match when lined up with each other - across the width of the carpet. It is not a quarter drop pattern, or a half drop pattern.

DROP PATTERN MATCH - The total pattern length has a number of pattern units in the repeat. To match the pattern the carpet must be shifted half or one quarter of the total pattern length. When the pattern is matched it creates a diagonal pattern.

SEAMING CAUTIONS

If hot glue drips on the top of the carpet when seaming don't try to wipe it off with your hand first as, you will burn yourself and second, you will smear it into the carpet. Let it dry and trim it off with scissors. Don't rush and accidents won't happen.

When using the iron set it on a scrap of carpet or pad. You don't want to take a chance of knocking it over and burning the carpet. Watch your hands when removing and returning the iron from the tray, hot glue can drip off of the bottom of the iron.

HAND SEWING SEAMS

In the past all seams were hand sewn with a **needle** and **thread,** today only certain carpets and specialty applications are hand sewn, almost all carpet is seamed using hot melt seam tape.

One reason to hand sew carpet is when a woven carpet is used that has a backing to which hot melt seam tape will not adhere. The carpet must have a secondary action backing to work well with hot melt seam tape. The common woven carpets are axminsters, wiltons, and velvets.

Another reason to hand sew carpet is in any situation in which the carpet is bent. These situation include; birdcage steps installed in a water fall fashion, and wrapping over ledges or steps.

Hot melt seams will open up if the carpet is bent in that area, while hand sewn seams are much less likely to.

THREADING THE NEEDLE

You need approximately one arms length of thread. This is around three foot of thread. Too much and you will have excess that make it difficult to work with.

A single thread is preferred over a double thread when hand sewing. Place enough thread through the needle eye so that it won't pull out of the needle when sewing.

A knot is tied in the end of the thread so that it won't pull through the carpet backing.

PATTERN MATCHING FOR A HAND SEWN SEAM

Hand sewing is done from the back of the carpet so you can not see the pattern when you are sewing.

You must lay the carpet out and match the pattern from the front. You then mark on each side of the carpet backing with a marker. When the carpet is folded over on its back, you then line up the marks that you placed on the back.

SEWING STYLES

To make it easier to push the needle through the backing at the correct depth when hand sewing the carpet, on a tube. A common tube to use is the cardboard tube from the center of the carpet roll.

PRACTICING THE STITCHES

The best way to learn the hand sewing stitches is to practice them. Below, I will give you some common stitches to practice. I suggest that you spend a day working with carpet scraps and practice sewing all of these stitches.

You can also learn to remember the stitches when away from the work area by drawing them. The advantage of this is that you can practice this any place, riding in the car on a trip or on a plane. This will not give you the real experience needed to work with the carpet and needle but only teach you to remember the stitches so that you remember them.

The start and finish of every seam is started with a lock stitch.

CROSS LOCK STITCH   WHIP LOCK STITCH

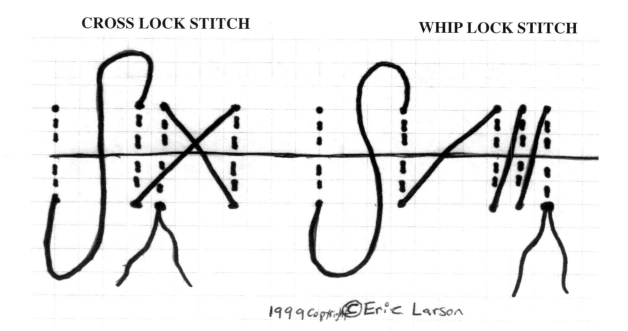

1999 copyright ©Eric Larson

TRAVELER STITCH - WHIP STITCH

TRAVEL AND LOCK STITCH

DOWN AND BACK STITCH - CROSS STITCH

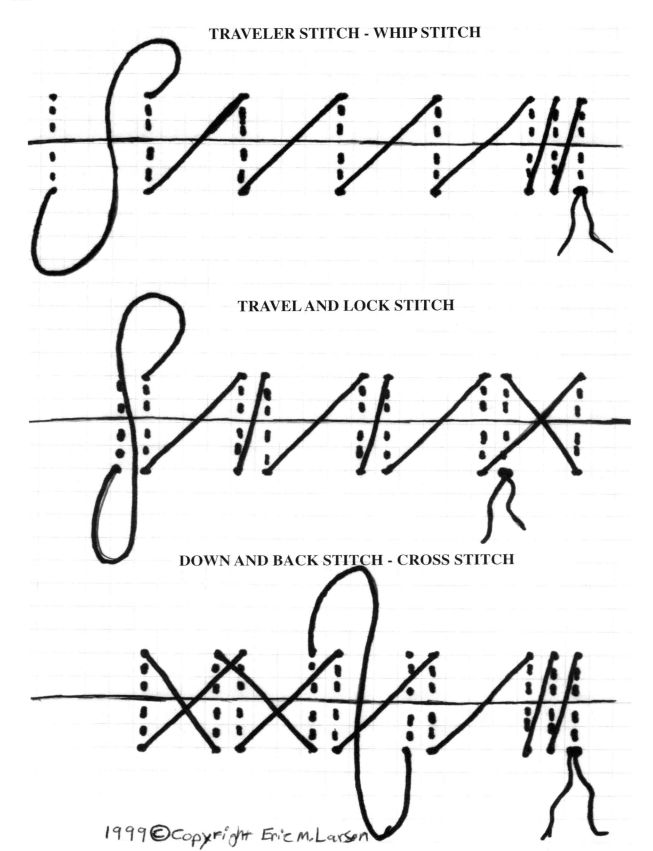

1999 ©Copyright Eric M. Larson

CROWS FOOT STITCH

CROWS FOOT AND BACK STITCH

AXMINSTER STITCH

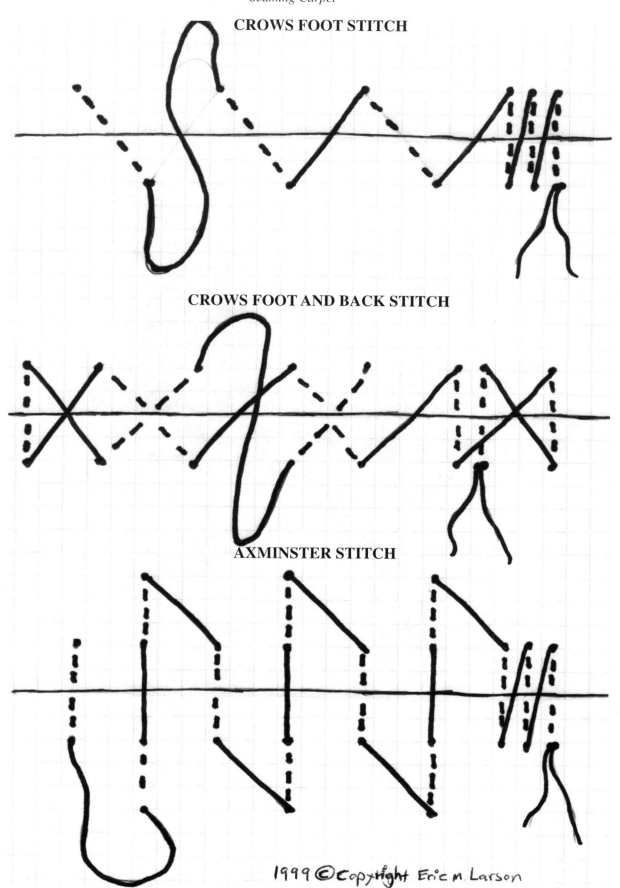

1999 ©Copyright Eric m. Larson

Thanks for an excellent job.

Did you remember to get the seam iron
out of the closet Jimmy Joe Bobby?

Uh duhh, is this the seam iron.
No, you moron! That's a hammer.

In the closet.

Fifteen minutes later, at the house.

You stupid ignoramise's!
You two don't know shit from shinola!

QUIZ - SECTION TWO
Seaming

1. You cut the edge of the carpet off for seaming using a?
(a) Row Cutter
(b) Straight edge
(c) Square
(d) All of the above

2. Cross seams are usually cut using a?
(a) Gillie Gun
(b) Trimmer
(c) Square
(d) Seam mate

3. What do you use to stick the carpet together with on seams?
(a) Duck tape
(b) Hot melt Seam tape
(c) Gillie Gun
(d) None of the above

4. Seaming is?
(a) Something that should be done very fast.
(b) Very important to the visuals of the job.
(c) Not very important
(d) Both a and c

5. When someone is putting a seam together you should?
(a) Walk on it to help it stick.
(b) Wait one minute before walking on it.
(c) Not walk on or near it until it has cooled.
(d) stop to answer the phone in the middle of seaming.

6. **T / F** Many times the room is wider than the width of the carpet, and will require a seam.

7. **T / F** Some carpets don't have straight rows and must to be straight -edged. Try row cutting first; you will be able to see if the rows are straight. Row cutting is the preferred method because you don't cut through any of the nap (pile) as when straight edging.

8. **T / F** The **tractor** is used to melt the glue on the seam tape.

9. **T / F** **Pressing the carpet into the glue quickly**, you don't want it to start drying. Use your hands and legs to push the carpet closer together or farther apart so that the backing is evenly together with no spaces or over laps.

10. **T / F** You have two flaps of carpet that need to be cut to make a doorway seam. One from each room.

11. **T / F** Rows do not always run both length ways and cross ways in all carpets, and when they do they usually are not square with each other. The square is usually most effective in this case.

12. **T / F** When using the iron set it on a scrap of carpet or pad.

13. **T / F** In the past all seams were hand sewn with a **needle** and **thread,** today things haven't changed much, most carpet still is hand sewn.

14. **T / F** Hot melt seams will open up if the carpet is bent in that area, while hand sewn seams will not as much.

15. **T / F** A single thread is preferred over a double thread when hand sewing. Place enough thread through the needle eye so that it won't pull out of the needle when sewing.

16. **T / F** Hand sewing is done from the back of the carpet so you can not see the pattern when you are sewing.

17. **T / F** To make it easier to push the needle through the backing at the correct depth when hand sewing, put the carpet on a tube. A common tube to use is the cardboard tube from the center of the paper towels.

18. **T / F** The best way to learn the hand sewing stitches is to practice them.

Answers   1. d   2. c   3. b   4. b   5. c 6. T
7. T   8. F 9. T 10. T 11. T 12. T 13. F 14. T
15. T 16. T 17. F 18. T

STEP TWELVE
STRETCHING THE CARPET

Pictured making a long stretch with the power-stretcher in a living room. When stretching the length you angle the stretcher to stretch more out of the width of the carpet.

Carpet must be stretched to achieve the proper tightness so that the carpet remains smooth and flat for its life. Carpet that is not stretched with a power stretch will develop wrinkles.

To assure that the carpet won't wrinkle, other factors also come into play. These factors are that the tack strip is of a good quality, it is wide enough, it has enough pins, it is not rotten, and it is the correct distance from the base boards.

Using tri tack tackstrip which has three rows of pins, and is an inch and one quarter wide, will ensure that the carpet stays hooked on the tack strip. Install the tack strip 3/8th of an inch from the baseboard, and renail any loose areas and ends without nails.

On rooms over 30' long always use a tri - tack with three rows of pins and renail if the tack strip does not come pre-nailed with inch long nails.

Power stretching and knee kicking are skills that require a little bit of practice to become good at. Practice stretching in a room in your home, or build a wood platform with different types of base boards to trim along each wall for practice.

THE POWER STRETCHER

Carpet is stretched using the **power-stretcher**. A power stretcher is a tool with tubes that span across the room and push against the **opposing** wall you are stretching away from. It has a head with teeth that hook on to the carpet

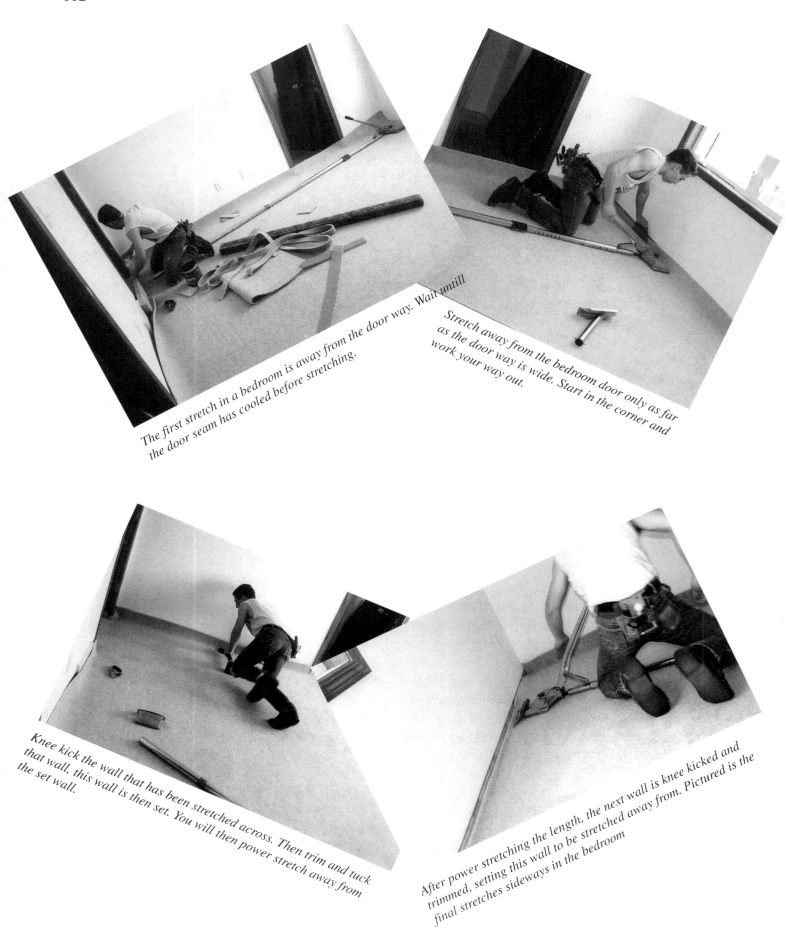

The first stretch in a bedroom is away from the door way. Wait untill the door seam has cooled before stretching.

Stretch away from the bedroom door only as far as the door way is wide. Start in the corner and work your way out.

Knee kick the wall that has been stretched across. Then trim and tuck that wall, this wall is then set. You will then power stretch away from the set wall.

After power stretching the length, the next wall is knee kicked and trimmed, setting this wall to be stretched away from. Pictured is the final stretches sideways in the bedroom and grip it. Keep the head of the stretcher just behind the tack strip when stretching.

The power stretcher handle is pushed down and uses leverage to stretch the carpet. With experience you can tell that you've stretched the carpet tight enough by how hard you are pressing down the power stretcher handle. This takes the experience of stretching many **types of carpets** and **room sizes** to know this by feel.

You can also tell if carpet is tight enough by some physical tests: *pulling up on the carpet nap (pile) and snapping it back to test for tightness.*

The larger a room is, the harder you will need to bear down on the power stretcher, this is because you are moving more carpet. The stiffer a carpet backing is, the more strength will be needed for you to push down on the stretcher handle.

The width of many rooms are normally narrower than the length and there is less carpet to stretch, so, **you will not need to stretch as hard in a small room (or shorter distance), as you would for a large one.** The more flexible the carpet backings are the easier they are to stretch, so go a little easier on these carpets when stretching.

If you over stretch you will pull the carpet off the **opposing wall slightly.** It doesn't take long to develop the experience to know how much you can stretch the carpet.

Tubes that span across the room are adjustable to four feet each. They push against the wall to stretch the carpet. Additional tubes can be purchased so that larger room sizes can be stretched.

A power stretcher comes with a foot to protect the wall you are stretching away from, but you will normally use a wider board placed along the opposite wall for additional protection.

KNEE KICKING

Some installers try to use the knee kicker to stretch the carpet in a large room, this will not stretch the carpet tightly enough to keep from wrinkling with time. Hard knee kicking

like this, trying and stretch in a large area, will damage your knees.

You can stretch in very small areas with a knee kicker, such as closets and areas no larger than 4' X 4'. For hallways, bathrooms, and walk in closets it may still be easier to use a power stretcher rather than to use a knee kicker, just go easier on power stretching these small areas. It's not very much carpet to stretch.

In very tight spaces that can not be knee kicked the carpet may need to be glued to the tack strip with a glue gun, and then trimmed and tucked. If the area is not very visible, or the carpet does not show staples, you may staple the carpet to the tack strip, **but only in these very tight spaces.**

The knee kicker is primarily used to set walls on to the tack strip, so it can be trimmed and tucked, then stretched away from this 'set area.' So, the knee kicker is used to hook the carpet on to the tack strip moving and placement of the carpet and some light stretching. It is also used for stretching the carpet on steps and very small closets.

SETTING A WALL

Carpet is set by hooking it on the tack strip with a knee kicker, then the area is trimmed and tucked so that the area can be power stretched away from.

A three foot area in one corner is set to

This wall was power stretched across. After stretching across a wall you knee kick the carpet to hook it on the tack strip. You then trim this wall to set it for stretching away from.

A six foot 2 x 4 is used for a stretcher board. This protects the wall.

make the first stretch away from.

Each wall that is power stretched across is then set. The wall that you stretch away from is called the set wall.

You **do not** cut down door ways on walls that are stretched across, until **after** you have stretched across the wall. This means that you **do not** set in, or make relief cuts for closets, door ways, and halls until after you stretch past the area.

STRETCHER BOARD

A board is used against the wall to protect the wall from the pressure of the power-stretcher pushing. You will want a 2 x 4 minimally and preferably a 2 x 6 thickness to protect the wall.

Various lengths of boards are used, long ones are for spanning across wide door ways, and short ones to fit between narrow areas that a long board won't fit into. A six foot length is most popular, it spans across the studs dispersing the pressure and assures that the wall won't be damaged.

Many installers carpet their stretcher boards for further protection of the wall.

ACCLIMATING CARPET

Acclimation, this means to lay out the carpet on the job site and leave it to condition at a room temperature between 65 ° - 95 ° degrees.

Acclimating carpet helps the carpet warm up and relax so that it will stretch properly. In cold weather, the carpet becomes very stiff, and it is especially important to allow the carpet to warm up before stretching it. Carpets with stiff backings require more acclimation time than a carpet backing that is relaxed and soft.

The Carpet and Rug Institutes standard time for acclimation is 48 hours, (at this time of writing).

Acclimating carpet for 48 hours is not practical in the real world of installation. Customers do not want to wait for two days, with their furniture moved out of the area, and installers do not want to start and leave a job to return later to install it.

Fortunately it is not necessary in most situations, and with most carpets, to acclimate carpet for this long. If the outdoor and indoor temperature are warm it probably is not necessary to acclimate carpet at all.

The standard method for acclimating carpet is to lay out the carpet in the house. Make sure the heat is between 65 ° - 95° degrees. Seam the carpet, then go to lunch for 1 hour before returning to stretch the carpet.

Power stretching up to the fire place tile in a living room. This is difficult to stretch up to, many installers prefer to set this area and to stretch away from it.

Power stretching down the length of the hallway up to a bedroom door. This door will need to be stay nailed to hold the stretch.

weight off the floor slightly so that you are not holding down the carpet. Use your body weight to move the carpet. Some installers try to knee kick the entire room in. This is hard on your knees and it does not ensure that the carpet will be tight enough. Very small areas such as walk in closets, can often be knee kicked in and be tight enough.

Installing carpet over carpet is not recommended. Such as stretching over a glue down carpet.

STRETCHING THE HALLWAY

You stretch the length of the hall with a power stretcher. The length can not be knee kicked and stretched tightly enough. Only if the hall is under 4' long is this an option at all, and then it will not work to kick up to doorways that are to be stay nailed.

* Stay nailing refers to placing nails through the carpet to temporarily hold the stretch in areas without tack strip installed, such as doorways

STRETCHING A ROOM

The tack strip can hold a lot of pressure so don't be shy about bearing down strongly and really stretching the carpet tightly. Ease back a little if the carpet is pulling away from the opposing wall. If you hear the wall creaking excessively ease back.

The first stretches of the wall are so important because they determine how hard you can stretch on all of the following stretches of that wall. A weak first stretch, and a harder second one, will cause the carpet to bubble up in the first stretch section.

Next, knee kick the carpet to hook it onto the tack strip so that it can be trimmed and tucked. Hold the head of the knee kicker approximately 1/2 - to 1 inches from the wall. Grip the knee kicker with your dominant hand. Hold down tightly so that it doesn't slide. The teeth will tear the carpet if you let the head of the knee kicker slide.

When knee kicking, lift your body

The sides of the hall may be stretched with the power stretcher, you don't need to stretch hard, because there isn't much carpet to

Stay nailing a bedroom doorway, after stretching down the hallway.

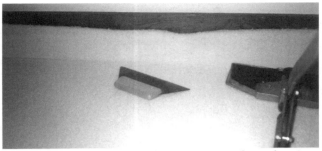

A spreader is used to press the carpet on to the tack strip when power stretching. Press hard dirctly into the gully.

move. Watch so that you don't pull the carpet off of the wall you are stretching away from, this often means that you're stretching too hard.

You may use the knee kicker, and place your foot against the wall for leverage, to stretch a hallway sideways.

When installing the hallway and bedrooms it is best to stretch the hall way in first, and then the bedrooms. I prefer not to stay nail hall doorways on the sides when I will be stretching away from that door way into the bedroom later. I believe you stretch the hallway more tightly sideways by power stretching into the bedroom. Seaming the bedroom doors is easier when they are not stay nailed. But you always need to stay nail the long length stretches in the hallway up to rooms that will be seamed on.

If the bedrooms are already installed and you are installing the hallway then you must stay nail the hall carpet and then seam the doors after stretching.

If you would stretch in the bedrooms prior to installing the hallway, then, you must stay nail the doors to hold the stretch. When the hallway is stretched in after the bed rooms you also must stay nail the hall doors prior to seaming.

USING A SPREADER

When power stretching the carpet is stretched, and then **held onto the tack strip with a tool called a spreader.** Press the spreader directly into the corner (gully). Press down hard into the gully and hold, then release the power stretcher while continuing to hold.

Move and stretch the next section and keep holding the previous stretch while you make the next stretch. **If you let off of the spreader when stretching** the next area it can release the stretch previously made.

TYPES OF CARPET AND THEIR STRETCH

How a carpet stretches is mostly determined by the type of backing. Different types of carpet backings require more tension to be stretched than others. Some types of carpets do not stretch in the width or length as much as others.

The thickness of the nap (pile density) can affect how easily a carpet bends and this affects how well it hooks to the tack strip.

A very thick plush carpet will not flex as well as a carpet with a thin nap (pile) and will not hook on to the tack strip as well, this can cause the carpet to release itself from the tack strip affecting the tightness of the stretch.

Power stretching sideways in a living room.

There are specific names for types of carpet backings:

JUTE BACK - This is a natural fiber backing, it looks like a burlap sack, and can be power stretched in both the width and the length. This is not a very common type of carpet backing anymore. The recommended stretch is 1% - 1 1/2% in the width and the length.

KANGA BACK and **ENHANCER BACKED** - These carpets have a padding attached and are not to be stretched.

UNTINARY - This backing is coated with a heavy latex. It normally does not have an action backing, but some times does. It is very stiff and is not recommended for power stretching.

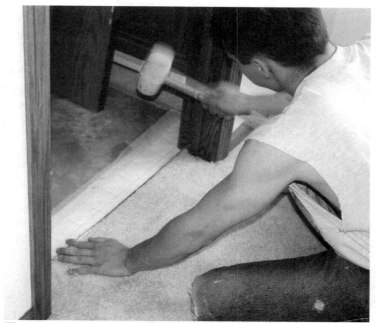

The carpet is cut into the metal, then hammering down, with a rubber mallet. You may need to kick extra carpet in to the metal when hammering it down. This assures that the carpet will never pull out of the metal

WOVEN GOODS - Woven goods are stretchable but some only stretch in the width or the length. **Axminsters** stretch mostly in the length and only slightly in the width. **Wiltons** stretch equally in the width and the length. **Velvets** stretch more in the width than in the length.

HOT MELT - This backing is coated with a heavy hot melt glue. It looks like plastic and is very stiff. Hot Melt backings are not to be power stretched.

ACTION BACKING - Action backed carpets have a secondary backing. It is a gridded mesh, usually white and coated with latex. These are the most common type of carpet today and are stretched in both the length and the width. The size of the mesh grids are rated by a size system called picks. This system uses the number of grids per inch. The recommended stretch is 1% - 1 1/2% in the width and the length.

SOFT BACK - Soft back carpet is normally an action backed carpet that is backed again with a soft fabric. This fabric prevents walls and base boards from being scratched. It stretches much the same as an action backed carpet. The recommended stretch is 1% - 1 1/2% in the width and the length.

You can tell how much a carpet will stretch by feeling the backing, a flexible backing will stretch more than a stiff one. Bending the carpet will tell you if it will stretch in that direction. Axminster carpets do not bend in the width, so they have very little stretch in the width.

You can tell how well a carpet is stretching by how easily the stretcher handle is to press down, and how much carpet stretches up the wall. A carpet that you really have to bear down on the stretcher handle to stretch is obviously very stiff. It also doesn't hook onto the tack strip as well.

Some carpets are not designed to stretch. These are non - stretchable carpets. These are kanga back carpets, enhancer backed carpets, carpets without backings, some unitary backed carpets and carpet tiles. If you are not sure of the installation method for a carpet check with the manufacturer.

SETTING CARPET INTO METALS

The carpet is cut and placed inside of the metal (under the lip) then, the lip is hammered down with a rubber mallet. A white rubber mallet is used so that black scuffs are not left.

STAY NAILING

Areas that need a stretch held temporarily are stay nailed. Stay nailing refers to placing nails through the carpet to temporarily hold the stretch in areas without tack strip installed, such as doorways.

It is not always necessary to stay nail all doorways, if you will be power stretching away from that area later. For example, a doorway on the side of a hallway that will be stretched away from. This will tighten the hall.

The hallway doorways are sometimes stay nailed to hold the stretch of the carpet. You always stay nail the doorways when installing a hallway, when the bedrooms are already installed.

A strip of carpet is used to nail through and nail into. Don't nail to deeply into the floor or the nails won't come out, the nails are only temporary.

You don't need to stay nail bedroom doors along the sides of the hallway if you will stretch the bedroom carpet afterwards. Stretching away from the bedroom door without stay nails, achieves a better stretch than if you stay nail.

It's best to stretch in a hallway first, and the bedrooms afterwards. This way you don't need to stay nail all of the doorways in most cases. If the bedrooms were installed prior to the hallway, then when installing the hallway the hall doorways will also need to be stay nailed.

Seaming with both doorways stay nailed can leave a little slack. Sometimes it must be done this way, but it is best to use stay nailing sparingly.

STRETCHING CARPET WITH A PIECE OF FURNITURE IN THE ROOM

You may eventually have to install carpet with for instance, a pool table in the basement. Suppose it is a slate pool table that was as-

Power stretching the length of the living room. He is angling it slightly.

sembled in the basement.

This will take a plan, so that you move it as little as possible. If you can put the table on furniture dollies and roll around this can help a lot.

You may start with the pool table in the center of the room to install tack strip. Then move it to one corner to pad. Once one side is padded you can move it to the other side, on top of the pad, to finish padding.

Next, lay out the carpet and stretch in as much as you can with the pool table in the corner. When you can no longer stretch anymore move the table to the opposite end of the room, on top of the stretched in carpet. Put it next to the wall as close as you can. You do not want it to hold down the carpet any more than is possible.

It takes a lot of moving but it can be done!

HOW TIGHT DO YOU STRETCH CARPET

The Carpet and Rug Institute standard for stretching an action or jute backed carpet is 1% -1 1/2% in the width and the length. You would need to do some calculations with the room size, and the amount of carpet that is stretching up the wall, to know if you are within this standard.

This standard does not take into account the large variations in each carpet backing. Some carpets can not be physically stretched this much with a power stretcher, they are simply to stiff and you could not physically push down on the stretcher handle this much. Other carpets will stretch much more than this.

This is why most installers use an instinctive method of power stretching along with some physical and visible tests on the carpet to check for tightness.

Most installers use an instinctive method of stretching,

this comes from experience of stretching in many types of carpets and room sizes. A stiffer carpet and a larger room will require you to press down harder on the stretcher handle to stretch the carpet. A soft, flexible backing, or smaller room size does not need to be stretched this hard. So, you can tell by how hard you are pushing down on the stretcher handle if you stretched the carpet enough.

Physical tests you can do to the carpet by pulling up on the nap (pile); it should snap back, this indicates that the carpet is tight.

Visibly you can see if the carpet is laying smooth, there should be no wrinkles or bubbles. A carpet that has gone loose and needs to be restretched will be visible obvious by the wrinkles in it.

You can also over stretch a carpet. If the carpet is pulling off of the opposing wall, then you may be stretching to hard. Keep an eye on the opposing wall for signs of pulling away.

Pulling away from a wall may also be a sign that the tack strip is not in good condition, or not attached with enough nails. If the tack strip is not attached well and is pulling up, then the carpet will not be tight enough, and will eventually wrinkle.

The closets are knee kicked in, and preferably power stretched away from. It may be too small of a space to kick in the sides, so it's ok to use the stapler (preferably a glue gun) to hold the carpet on to the tack strip. The closets are not a real visably noticable area so this can be done, but knee kick the sides in if possible.

The Carpet Installation Training Handbook

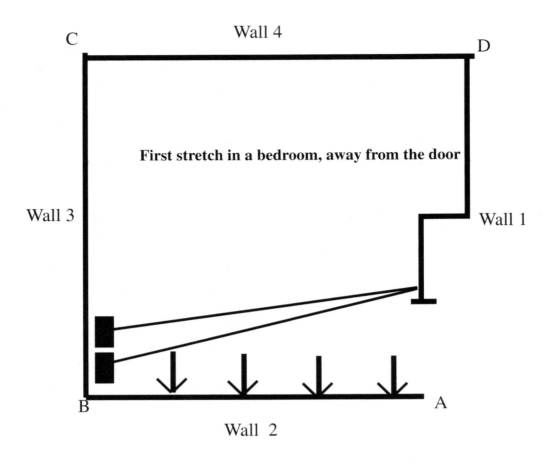

First stretch in a bedroom, away from the door

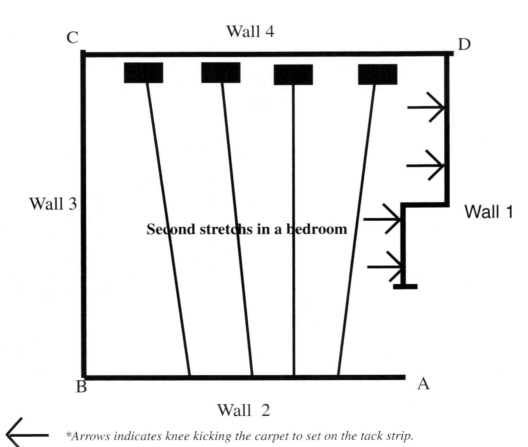

Second stretchs in a bedroom

Arrows indicates knee kicking the carpet to set on the tack strip.

POWER STRETCHING DIRECTIONS

Learning power stretching directions of every type of room requires a lot of time on many different jobs. After awhile you'll have seen every type of layout. Normally you should set in more difficult areas such as curved metals and then power-stretch away from them.

Develop a method for each layout and use the same method each time.

The power stretching directions for a patterned carpet are more complex. This is because the pattern must stay straight in the room.

* The stretching directions shown in the diagrams, are typical of most unpatterned carpets.

POWER STRETCHING A BEDROOM

These are typical stretching directions of most installers, but if you are working for someone, follow the instructions of the installer you are working for.

The first stretch in a bedroom is usually made away from the doorway after the seam has cooled. This is for most bedrooms with a hallway that is seamed on. When stretching away from the door you angle the power stretcher, because the carpet tends to shift away from wall # 2. The first stretch is very important because it pulls and stretches the hallway.

The first stretch you make determines how much you will be able to stretch the remainder of the wall. This determines how tight all of the following stretches will be and how tightly the final room is stretched. If you make a light stretch for the first one and try to stretch harder on following stretches it will cause a bubble. Stretch from corner (a) to corner (b) no farther than the width of the doorway.

After stretching across a wall, you set it by knee kicking the carpet onto the tack strip, then trim and tuck the wall. So now knee kick

wall #2 to hook it on the tack strip. Knee kicking tightens the slack out of the carpet and stretches the carpet some. Having the carpet hooked on to the strip well makes it easier to trim accurately. If it is not hooked on the strip well it can bubble when tucking.

Finish setting wall # 2 by trimming and tucking the carpet. Hold one hand on the tack strip simultaneously as you are tucking, this keeps the carpet from popping off of the strip when tucking. You will stretch away from wall #2 and that will pull out any bubbles if any occur. If the baseboard is raised 1/2 inch off of the floor you can trim the carpet longer.

The second stretch is from corner (a) to wall #4 near corner (d.) Angle the power stretcher on the first stretch, as this helps to keep the carpet from shifting away from wall #1. The first stretch on the second wall is important because its the first stretch of this wall and all the following stretches can only be as tight as this one. Continue stretching all the way across wall #4. Start to angle toward corner c as you are stretching. Angling this way helps to pull out any slack towards wall #3. Knowing when to angle and when to keep the stretcher straight is vital to avoiding wrinkles.

Next knee kick wall #1 and then trim and tuck it. Now wall #1 is set and ready to stretch away from.

The final wall to finish power stretching towards is wall #3. Stretch from wall #1 to wall #3, where you stopped stretching away from the door way, and continue stretching down the wall to corner c. Keep the power stretcher straight. You do not want to angle towards wall #4, or you will stretch more carpet towards it and force a bubble next to wall #4. Its already trimmed and tucked so it doesn't need to be stretched more.

Next trim and tuck wall #3. The room is completely stretched now!

The final step is to cut out any floor registers. To cut a floor register feel the floor to locate it. Press firmly on the carpet until you find it. You will want a new knife blade to top cut through the carpet. Then cut an X in the center of the vent. Continue cutting until you see the edge

The Carpet Installation Training Handbook

The final stretchs in a bedroom

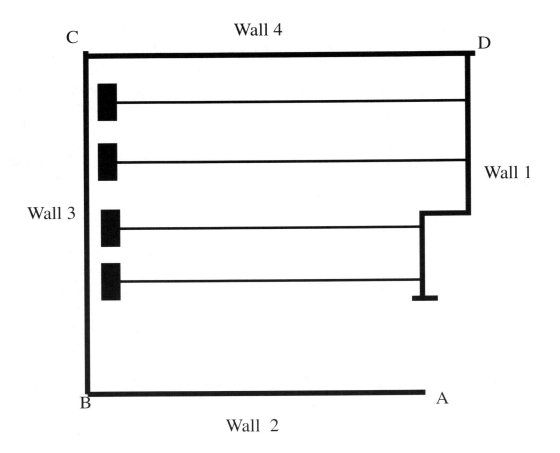

Arrow indicates knee kicking the carpet to set it on the tack strip.

of the floor and cut all around the vent. **This completes the stretching of the bedroom.**

CARPETING BATH ROOMS

A trick to stretching in small areas like bathrooms, is, to use extra tack strip in tight places. Behind the toilet you completely line the area with tack strip. No one walks behind the toilet and you need something to staple to. Double the tack strip under the toe kick so that it's easier to hook onto.

Use the power stretcher for the first long stretch into the bath room. You may or may not be able to use the power stretcher to stretch sideways. This depends on what you have to stretch off of and how large the room is.

But **if you do use the power stretcher go easy on a small room.** You can usually use the foot of the stretcher to stretch away from the toilet. You may not be able to stretch off of the toe kicks so in this case use the knee kicker to stretch sideways.

Set the most difficult areas first, under the toe kick and around the toilet.

To install around a toilet kick straight back on each side with the knee kicker. The sides are too narrow of an area to kick. So use the hot melt glue gun and glue the carpet down on the tack strip.

Sometimes the wall trimmer can be used for straight cuts around the toilet. This won't work for rounded places around the toilet, so fold back the carpet and hand cut these areas with a knife.

Do not use extra tack strip in front of the bath tub because the pins can stick through and poke bare feet.

The most difficult situation in a bathroom is installing around the toilet.

A bath room prior to carpeting. Check all of the tack strip and replace any that is bad. Line behind the toilet with tack strip, and double strip the sides around the toilet. Double strip under the toe kicks.

Pictured is the finished bath room carpeted.

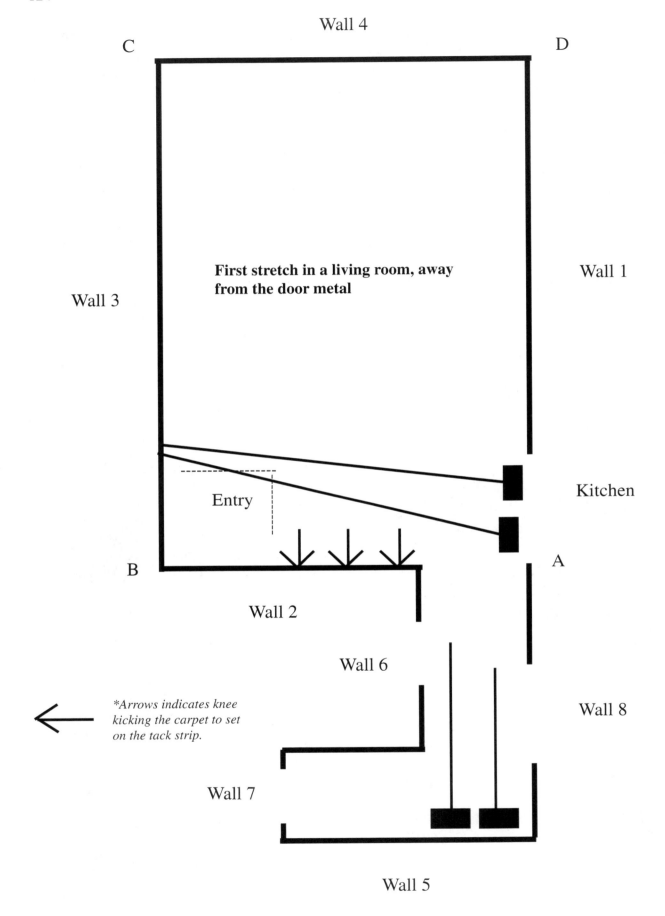

Wall 4

C   D

First stretch in a living room, away from the door metal

Wall 3

Wall 1

Kitchen

Entry

B   A

Wall 2

Wall 6

Arrows indicates knee kicking the carpet to set on the tack strip.

Wall 8

Wall 7

Wall 5

Kick in the closets with the knee kicker.

A toilet prior to carpeting. Remove any rotten tack strip. Double the tack strip on the sides and line the back completely with tack strip, so that you can glue the carpet to the tack strip.

TIPS TO STRETCHING IN TIGHT AREAS

This is an area such as the sides of small closets, very small closets, or around a toilet. These areas don't need to be stretched real tight, but, if they are not attached to the tack strip before tucking then the carpet will bubble up.

You can not use a knee kicker in these areas so you must glue or staple the carpet down to the tack strip, prior to trimming, and tucking it.

With a glue gun you run a bead of glue on to the tack strip, then push the carpet onto the tack strip. Use a seam roller to keep pushing it onto the tack strip until the glue dries. The advantage of using a glue gun is that no staples will show, or rust. This **may not** be important in some very small closets, but **it is** in a bath room.

The other solution is to use the gilli gun to staple the carpet on to the tack strip. Spread the nap (pile) apart when stapling, so as not to staple the nap down with the staples. Staples are not recommended in highly visible areas because they can show dimples in the carpet. This will vary with the type of carpet you are installing.

POWER STRETCHING A LIVING ROOM & HALL

The stretching directions shown in the diagrams are typical of most installers, but if you are working for some one, follow the directions of the installer you are working for.

First decide on which corner to set and stretch away from. Theoretically you can start from any corner, but it's easier for you to start from a specific area. **I set the more difficult areas first.** In this case I would rather set the

The finished toilet with carpet installed.

Second stretchs in a living room

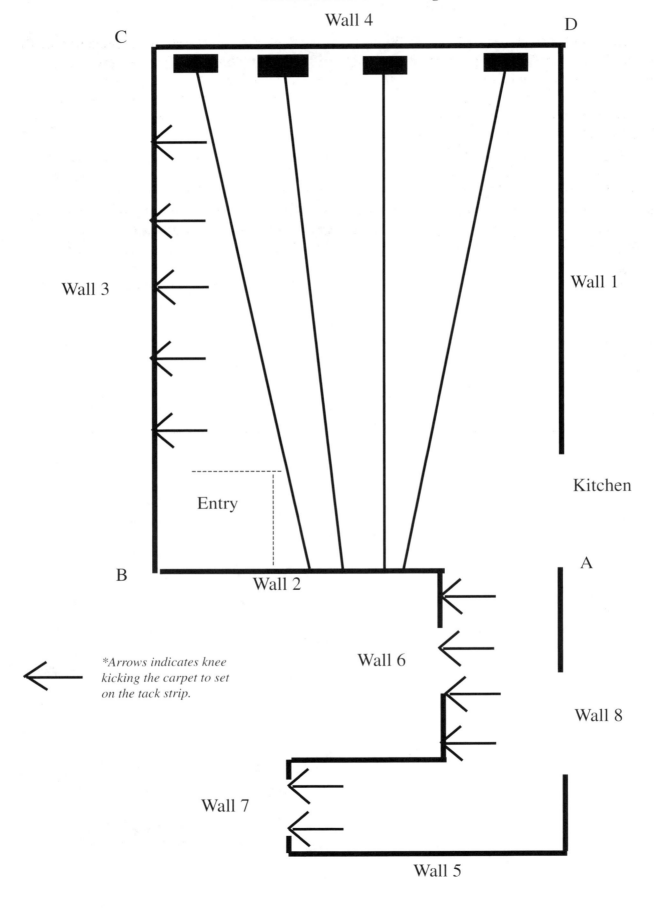

Arrows indicates knee kicking the carpet to set on the tack strip.

entry metal than to stretch into it. I almost always stretch away from curved metals. A wall with a lot of angles is easier to kick with the knee kicker rather than to stretch into it. If you have a 12 foot doorway, you probably will not have a board long enough to span the length of it to stretch. I stretch into long metals like this.

Keep stretching the carpet in the same directions that you start if possible, don't try switching directions mid stream. In this case the carpet is all being stretched towards wall #1 and wall #4, but it will be back stretched down the hall, this is the exception to keeping it going the same direction. You will always stretch down the hallway regardless of the direction you are stretching the living room.

There are some other situations in which you back stretch carpet, and this depends on the layout of the room. This is a decision you must make when deciding the stretching directions you will use. Take into consideration whether back stretching will cause the carpet to bubble.

Start by, cutting the carpet around the entry metal. Use one hand to hold the carpet tight against the metal and top cut through using the metal as a guide. Cut on the outer edge of the metal to leave more carpet under the lip of the metal. Use the tucker to set the carpet under the metal lip. It may be necessary to kick into the metal, to force more carpet into the metal. Then hammer it down evenly.

For the first stretches, power stretch away from the entry door metal into the kitchen metal. From corner (b) to corner (a), up to wall #1. Stretch no further than the width of the entry metal.

Locking the stretch in place to cut the metal. Set carpet in the metal the width of the power stretcher head. Using the back of the metal as a guide for cutting. Tuck about half of the distance of what you cut under the metal lip and hammer that down evenly using the rubber mallet .You only tuck and hammer down half because the second stretch can overlap pulling the carpet in the previously stretched area more and causing a bubble.

After stretching across wall #2, you knee kick wall #2 on to the tack strip. Then trim and tuck the carpet to set the wall. You will be stretching away from wall #2 after it is set.

Next, power stretch down the hall way to wall #5. A two by four is placed between the doorways, or you can stretch from wall #4, but this will take a lot of tubes. Once stretched the end of the hall can be trimmed and tucked.

Knee kick, trim and tuck wall #6 in the hallway. You may want to power stretch towards wall #7. Trim and tuck wall #6 all the way across wall #6 and #7 is now set.

For the second stretches, power stretch away from wall #2 to corner (c.) Work your way all the way across wall #4 to corner (d.) Then trim and tuck wall #4.

Next knee kick, trim and tuck wall #3 in the living room. Now wall #3 is set and ready to stretch away from.

For the final living room stretches, take the power stretch all of the way back to where you left off from stretching away from the entryway. Stretch away from wall #3 up to wall #1. Stretch all the way across wall #1 to corner (d), keeping the power stretcher straight. Work your way to the corner (d) to finish the living room. Then trim and tuck wall #1. The living room is completely finished.

Next finish the hallway by stretching away from wall #6 toward wall #8. You could set wall #8 instead, and power stretch towards wall #6 and #7, if you prefer. It will work either way. When using the power stretcher to stretch a short distance like this you don't need to bear down too much, you are only stretching a small amount of carpet in the width of the hallway.

The final step is to cut out any registers. To cut a floor register, feel the floor for it. Press firmly on the carpet until you find it. You will want a new knife blade to top cut through the carpet. Then cut an X in the center of the vent. Continue cutting until you see the edge of the floor and cut all around the vent.

This concludes the stretching directions of a living room.

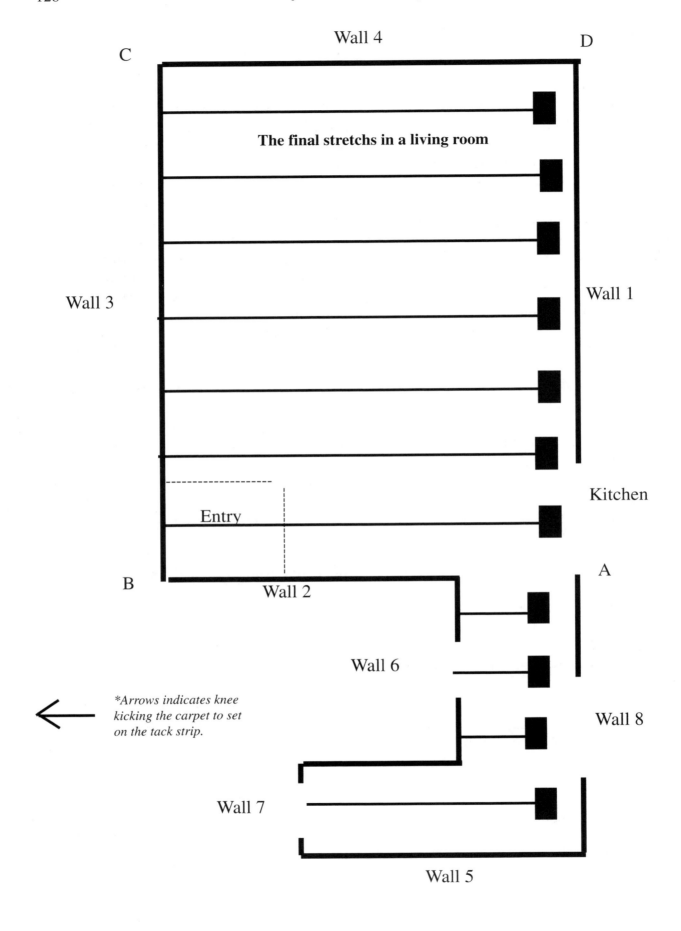

Wall 4

C

D

The final stretchs in a living room

Wall 3

Wall 1

Kitchen

Entry

A

B

Wall 2

Wall 6

Wall 8

Arrows indicates knee kicking the carpet to set on the tack strip.

Wall 7

Wall 5

TIPS TO POWER STRETCHING

⇒ Make sure that the first stretch of the wall is adequate in that the tightness of all the following stretches are determined by this. If the first stretch is not tight than that area will bubble up on the following stretch.

⇒ If possible, stretch in a direction which you set the more difficult areas in with the knee kicker, and stretch away from those areas.

⇒ Don't try to make your stretch all in one bite, when pushing down on the power stretcher handle make two or three smaller bites, rather than all in one big stretch. You also start with the stretcher handle half way down rather than all of the way up.

⇒ Continue holding the previous stretch in place with the spreader when making the next stretch. The previous stretch will come loose of the tack strip if you don't do this.

⇒ Do not make corner cuts, closet cuts, or doorway cuts until after stretching past that wall, if at all possible. You may have to make some corner cuts, but keep these to a minimum.

STRETCHING A PATTERNED CARPET

You must be much more careful about keeping the carpet straight in the room when it has a pattern. If it should run up one wall more than another then it will look crooked in the room. It is difficult to get a patterned carpet to line up straight with a wall and leave 2 - 3 inches of extra carpet up the wall. It is also difficult to stretch the carpet and keep it straight in the room.

When laying out the carpet line up one side with the longest, most visible wall in the room. Measure the room for squareness, to make sure that the walls them selves are straight.

To get the carpet pattern straight with the wall you must make triangle cuts into the pattern along the edge of the carpet. Make 3 - 4

cuts along a wall, then line these cuts up straight with the wall to be stretched across.

To stretch a patterned carpet, you stretch across the longest straight wall, so that it stays straight. Then set this wall, so that you know it is straight. You then stretch away from this wall. Avoid angling the power stretcher as this could shift the carpet out of square. Stretch evenly and straight and the carpet should stay straight in the room.

Pay close attention to laying out the carpet straight to begin with and you will most likely prevent having any problems when stretching.

REASONS FOR CARPET WRINKLING

♦ *INCORRECT STRETCHING DIRECTION AND PROCEDURES*

♦ *BACK STRETCHING, STRETCHING BACK INTO AN AREA THAT IS ALREADY TUCKED*

♦ *NOT STRETCHING HARD ENOUGH ON THE FIRST STRETCHES OF THE WALL*

♦ *NOT STRETCHING THE CARPET TIGHTLY ENOUGH*

♦ *ALLOWING THE CARPET TO POP OFF OF THE STRIP WHEN TUCKING IT IN*

♦ *NOT ATTACHING THE TACK STRIP SECURELY ENOUGH*

♦ *NOT REPLACING ROTTEN TACK STRIP*

♦ *NOT ATTACHING THE METALS WITH ENOUGH NAILS*

♦ *DEFECTIVE CARPET*

♦ *THE CARPET BEING PULLED LOOSE FROM THE TACK STRIP BY A CUSTOMER OR OTHERS*

RESTRETCHING CARPET

This is the stretching of carpet that had previously been stretched in, but needs to be stretched again because it has wrinkled.

Carpet wrinkles for various reasons such as: not stretching it enough, knee kicking the carpet in instead of power stretching it, defective carpet, wet shampooing the carpet, very high humidity, poor quality of tack strip, and trying to stretch in a carpet that is not manufactured for a stretch in installation.

Carpet will go loose if it is pulled off of the tack strip, for repairs, or remodeling, and not restretched. **If carpet was installed with 1/4** round not removed, this could cause the carpet to come loose of the tack strip and go loose.

Carpet can go loose if the tack strip is in poor quality, and not replaced at the installation time. This could mean that the tack strip was rotten, not a wide heavy brand, or not nailed in well enough.

You generally try to only pull the carpet loose from two walls when restretching a room. Try to leave the carpet in the metals and difficult areas as much as possible. If possible, do n*o*t tear or cut apart seams to restretch carpet.

When restretching **you will stretch past registers** and need to patch a piece in. Use a piece of seam tape, and the glue gun. There will be enough extra carpet that trims off of the walls.

For restretching a hallway you can stretch away from it in the living room and stretch down it also. You may need to stretch into the bedrooms to tighten the hallway, or you may have to reseam the door ways. Stretching into the bedroom takes less time, and does less damage than reseaming.

Sometimes carpet needs to be repaded and restretched. This could be because the padding has gone bad, (foam pad breaking down and powdering) or, flood damage in which the pad needs to be removed and new installed. Do not tear any seams apart unless its absolutely necessary. In order to fold back the carpet, cutting loose some seams may be necessary in door ways. Fold the carpet over, and repad one side at a time, then restretch the carpet.

STRETCHING IN A TRAILER

Many trailer homes do not have walls that are constructed as strongly as a normal home. If you are in doubt of the strength of any wall, press against the lower wall using your foot before stretching.

Most of these homes can still be stretched using the power stretcher. Put a 2 x 4 at least six feet long against the wall you are stretching away from. The power stretcher pushes with tremendous pressure and the board will disperse this over a large enough area to protect the wall. Begin pushing on the stretcher handle lightly to make sure the wall is holding solid. A board should be used in all homes for protecting the wall. Place it along the lower wall to stretch off of. This ensures that you won't damage any walls.

In a worst case situations, the carpet would have to be knee kicked throughout the trailer. In this case, make sure the carpet used has a flexible enough backing that it can be kicked tightly enough and stay tight. Also use a tack strip that will really grip when you have to knee kick, like a tri tack with three rows of pins.

MULTIPLE CHOICE QUIZ
Section 2
Stretching the carpet

1. You protect the wall from the foot of the power stretcher with?
    (a) A 2 x 4 that is 4-6 foot long.
    (b) You don't need to protect the wall.
    (c) Your Tool Box
    (d) Foam rubber

2. You stretch carpet with a power stretcher because?
    (a) The knee kicker doesn't ensure it will be tight enough.
    (b) You want it to stay wrinkle free for its life.
    (c) Both a and b.
    (d) None of the above

3. When power stretching you hold the carpet on to the tack strip using a?
    (a) Hammer and Nails
    (b) Seam Iron
    (c) Spreader
    (d) Spackaler

4. Normally you power stretch away from?
    (a) Difficult areas
    (b) Curved Metal
    (c) a & b
    (d) twelve foot wide metals

5. When you restretch carpet you.....
    (a) may need to stretch into the bedrooms to tighten the hallway
    (b) do not tear apart doorway seams, its usually not necessary
    (c) you must cut all of the seams apart
    (d) both a and b

TRUE / FALSE -QUIZ
Section 2
Stretching the carpet

6 . **T / F** A trick to stretching in small areas like bathrooms, is, to use extra tack strip in tight places.

7. **T / F** A stiffer carpet, and a larger room will require you to press down harder on the stretcher handle to stretch the carpet.

8. **T / F** Stay nailing refers to placing nails through the carpet to temporarily hold the stretch in areas without tackstrip installed such as doorways.

9. **T / F Carpet must never be stretched** to achieve the proper tightness so that the carpet remains smooth and flat for its life.

10. **T / F Using tri tack tack strip which has three rows of pins,** and is an inch and one quarter wide, will ensure that the carpet stays hooked on the tackstrip.

11. **T / F You can also tell if carpet is tight enough by some physical tests:** *pulling it off of the tack strip and checking the back to test for tightness.*

12. **T / F Carpet is set by hooking it on the tack strip with a knee kicker,** then the area is trimmed and tucked so that the area can be power stretched away from.

13. **T / F If you would stretch in the bedrooms prior to installing the hallway,** then, you must stay nail the doors to hold the stretch.

14. **T / F** When power stretching, the carpet is stretched, and then **held onto the tack strip with a tool called a knee kicker.**

15. **T / F The Carpet and Rug Institute standard for stretching an action or jute backed carpet is 1% -1 1/2% in the width and the length.**

16. **T / F You can also over stretch a carpet.** If the carpet is pulling off of the apposing wall, then you may be stretching to hard.

17. **T / F** The power stretching directions for a patterned carpet are easier. This is because the pattern must **not** stay straight in the room.

18. **T / F** Make corner cuts, closet cuts, or doorway cuts before stretching past that wall, if at all possible.

19. **T / F Carpet wrinkles for various reasons** such as: not stretching it enough, knee kicking the carpet in instead of power stretching it, defective carpet, wet shampooing the carpet, very high humidity, poor quality of tack strip, and trying to stretch in a carpet that is not manufactured for a stretch in installation.

20. **T/F The thickness of the nap (pile) can affect how easily a carpet bends and this affects how well it hooks to the tack strip.**

Answers
1. a 2. c 3. c 4. c 5. d 6. T 7. T 8. T
9. F 10. T 11. F 12. T 13. T 14. F 15. T
16. T 17. F 18. F 19. T 20. T

That walls really creaking. Creek, creeek, sqeeek, crrreeeek.

Oh, thats just the power stretcher squeeking.

Crreeek, squeek, creeek - curraashhhhh

STEP THIRTEEN
TRIMMING AND TUCKING

Trimming and tucking the carpet are very important to the quality of the finished job.

Trimming the carpet to the right length so that it tucks in smoothly is essential. In most situations the trimmer handle is kept straight up and down. *Always keep the trimmer pushed tightly against the wall.*

If the baseboards are set up off the floor so there is space for the carpet to be tucked under, then you can trim the carpet longer. This is done by turning the handle outward farther away from the wall.

If there is less space to tuck the carpet; then it needs to be trimmed shorter.

Start with the trimmer handle straight up and down and if it needs to be trimmed shorter or longer adjust your trimming by turning the handle farther in or out.

Corners, that cannot be trimmed with the trimmer are cut by using a carpet knife. Fold the carpet down and cut it from the back estimating the proper length. When folding the last bit back to cut it, be careful that the carpet does not pull off of the tack strip.

Use new trimmer blades on each job and change them whenever they become dull. There are two sides to the blades. They can be turned to use the other side that is not dull.

If the carpet is trimmed too short then you can use the power stretcher to stretch it up a little closer. It's best to cut it right the first time and save yourself a lot of time.

USING A WALL TRIMMER

• *To trim shorter turn the trimmer handle in towards the wall.*

• *To trim longer turn the trimmer handle out farther towards the room.*

• *For typical trimming length keep the trimmer handle straight up and down.*

• *Keep the trimmer pressed firmly against the wall.*

• *Watch the length you are trimming the carpet as you are trimming it and adjust the length as needed.*

Pictured using excellent form trimming the carpet using the wall trimmer. Notice the wall trimmer won't trim all the way into the corners, this is cut with the carpet knife.

The wall trimmer is used to trim the carpet next to walls, next to fire place mantles, tile, wood floors, base boards of all heights and all sorts of walls. You must know the correct length to trim the carpet in all situations, depending on what you are trimming next to. Getting the correct length is essential when trimming so that the carpet will tuck easily, will look good and so that it is under the wall enough so that it does not pull away when power stretching.

Pictured tucking the trimmed carpet along the wall for a smooth finished look. He is using a plastic safety tucker, that prevents the possibility of scratching the woodwork.

TUCKING THE CARPET

You **tuck the carpet by pressing down on the cut edge of the carpet** using a tucker. This pushes the carpet into the gully. (The space between the wall and the tack strip.)

Then **run the tucker with a scraping motion along the baseboard to make a smooth crease.** Force any threads still sticking up into the gully or cut them off.

Sometimes the carpet doesn't want to stay hooked on the tack strip when you are tucking it. You should then use your opposite hand to simultaneously hold the carpet on the strip while tucking.

Any **loose strings sticking up from the edges should be cut off with a knife** or tucked in. A well done trimming and tucking job makes the difference between a professional looking job and a hack job.

METALS

A nap lock pin metal is almost always used instead of a flat bar metal. Flat bars are only used when their is a height difference too great to use a pin metal. The pin metals are installed when the tack strip is installed and a flat bar metal is installed after the carpet is installed.

You **trim the carpet into a pin metal** by holding the edge of the carpet tightly against the metal with one hand and top cutting through the carpet. Use the outer edge of the metal lip as a guide to run your knife along. Tuck the carpet in under the lip and then hammer the lip down with a rubber mallet. Hammer smoothly and evenly so that the metal lip is hammered down uniformly.

Tucking the carpet along the firepace mantle using a vinyl knife. A vinyl knife is often used for tucking carpet; it's narrow edge works well for presision tucking into tight spaces.

After trimming the carpet the cut edge is tucked in along the wall. When tucking the carpet hold one hand next to the area you are tucking in to keep the carpet from coming loose off the tack strip. Tuck all of the carpet uniformly so that it looks good. Cut off any loose strings that don't tuck in.

A curved metal can be used to finish off the carpet next to wood or vinyl. The carpet is cut to the metal, tucked in and the lip of the metal hammered down with a rubber mallet.

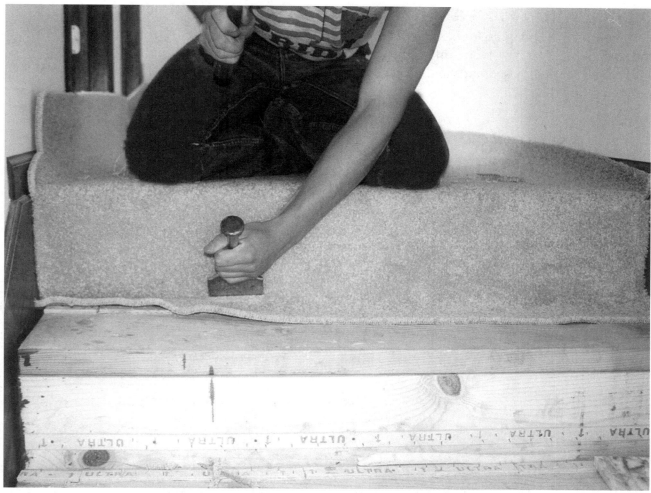

The stair tool and hammer are used to set carpet over the top step riser. The sides of the carpet must be trimmed to just the right width to fit over the top riser before setting it into place.

If you are using a flat bar metal the carpet is cut evenly to where the metal is to be placed. The edge of the carpet is stapled down then the metal is nailed down over the carpet edge. Use nails to match the metal color.

On concrete, if a flat bar metal is used they are drilled through the pre-made holes. Nail anchors are placed into the drilled holes so that nails can be hammered into the holes drilled and will hold the metal. Be very careful when drilling near a berber carpet, if the drill catches the yarns it will run across the carpet. Metals come in gold and silver colors.

SETTING OVER STEPS

Use the stair tool and a hammer to set the **carpet over the top step**. Push the carpet over the top step using the knee kicker and pushing against your chest. Simultaneously hammer the carpet between the stair tack strip in the area that you are stretching. Cut off the excess carpet using a carpet knife.

FLOOR REGISTERS

Registers are cut through the top of the carpet by slicing an X in the center, then cutting around the edges. Use a new knife blade so that the cut is not frayed.

Make sure that all floor registers have been cut out. You can feel them by crawling around the perimeter of the room and pressing with your hand.

BASEBOARD TYPES & THEIR TRIMMING APPLICATIONS

Every type of baseboard has a different trimming method that is used. Different jobs and even the same job may have several different types of baseboards and trimming applications.

Some types of baseboards and quarter round are not recommended for carpet installation without removing them.

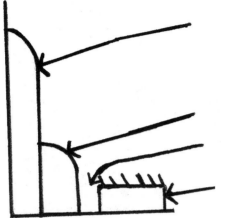

This baseboard is installed with quarter round. This quarter round is high enough to trim next to like a normal wall. The tack strip is installed 3/8th of an inch back.

Baseboards are installed flat on the floor.
A 3/8th inch gully is left for tucking. The trimmer is held straight up and down for the trimming length. It must be accurate. Tack strip is installed 3/8th of an inch back.

The Wall has no baseboard installed but it will be installed after installation. The gully is left wide to allow for the baseboard to be installed after the installation. Keep the tack strip held back the thick ness of the hammer head. The trimmer is held straight up and down. The baseboard will cover the cut edge.

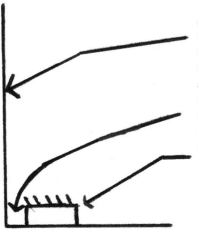

No baseboards will be installed. The tack strip is held back 3/8th of an inch as usual.
A standard gully size is used. Trimming is accurate. Hold the trimmer straight up and down.

The baseboard is held up 1/2 inch to allow extra space for tucking this makes a better edge. Trim longer so that the carpet is tucked under the base. The tack strip is held back a normal 3/8 of an inch.

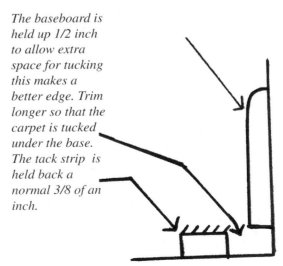

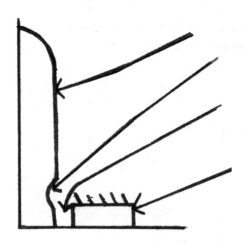

This baseboard has a notch in it, it makes for difficult trimming and tucking.

Hold the trimmer straight up and down.

The tack strip is installed a normal 3/8th of an inch back from the baseboard.

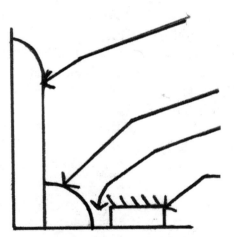

The baseboard is installed with quarter round.

Quarter round was never intended to be used with carpet, it is for covering the edge around the room on vinyl or hard wood floors.

The quarter round is low and rounded, this is not recommended for carpet installation as the carpet tends not to stay tucked. None the less if you must install with it, you will turn the trimmer inward and trim shorter. The tack strip is installed a normal 3/8th of an inch back.

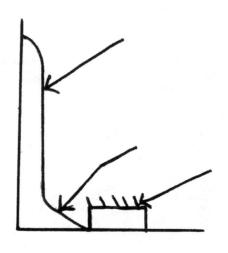

This is not a very common type of baseboard,, it is rounded at the bottom, making it impossible to tuck the carpet.

This type of baseboard is not intended for use with carpet.

It was made as an all in one base with quarter round for hard wood floors or vinyl flooring.

Pictured is a hallway with all the left over scraps from trimming. They will be picked up in trash bags and carried out by the van.

STEP FOURTEEN
PICKING UP SCRAPS AND TOOLS

Picking up the scraps is done as you are working and at the end of the job.

Set all the scraps outside by the side of the van. Remember that the tools need to be loaded in the van first and then the scraps.

Keep the carpet and pad scraps separated so that the pad scraps can be recycled. Don't throw anything else in with the pad such as carpet, dirt, tack strip, or metal pieces.

Clean pad, (new and used), can be **recycled** to help the environment. Most cites have a pad recycling program that pays cash for pad.

LOOKING FOR ANYTHING LEFT BEHIND

As you are picking up scraps look for any tools hidden under scraps. As you are working, always put all tools back near the tool box when you are finished using them. To avoid loosing tools, *never set tools on counters , shelves or ledges.*

VACUUMING

Vacuum after the job is completed for a 100% finished look. Pick up all small scraps so that the vacuum is not clogged. Use a heavy duty commercial vacuum. Also use an edger to vacuum around the edges of the room.

PATCHING NICKS IN WOODWORK

This is a good time to **notice if there are any nicks and scratches in the woodwork caused from the installation.** I carry several types of colored wood putty (various colors) for patching any larger nicks.

Most often they are only scuff marks and disappear with a quick wiping with Old English Oil. I carry Old English wood oil in three colors to rub on the different colors of wood work if it is scuffed up.

STEP FIFTEEN
LOADING ALL TOOLS AND SUPPLIES

As you are working **set the tools that you are finished with back next to your tool box** so they're not scattered throughout the house. Never set tools up on window ledges, shelves in closets, or counter tops. This ensures that you will not lose any tools and makes it easier to pick up at the end of a job.

Load all of the tools into their proper location in the tool boxes. Set all of the tools and supplies near the door to be carried out. Carry all of the tools out and put them in their proper locations in the van so that they can be found for the next job.

During snow or rainy conditions you will want to lay a scrap of pad or carpet by the doorway to wipe your feet on as you carry in and out.

Always **walk through the job for a final**

All of the tools are gathered up and repacked into the tool boxes after the job is finished. Take a good look around for any tools that could be left.

Pictured throwing away the bags of carpet scraps into the dumpster. All of the pad scraps are taken to a recycling center.

look to make sure nothing was forgotten. Check for forgotten tool, check for registers that didn't get cut out and look over the entire job for anything that you may have missed.

Load your tools into the van **first** before loading trash bags and old carpet pad that is to be hauled away. The tools need to be under the trash so that the trash can be unloaded.

Make sure that *everything* to do in the home is completely done before loading the tools, or you will need to unload them again.

INVENTORY OF YOUR SUPPLIES

Take an inventory of any supplies that you are running low on. Such as tack strip, carpet blades, staples, and metals. So that you

Pictured unloading the trash from the van after the job. Keep the van clean so that it's ready for the next job.

are prepared for the next job. Write your list on a piece of paper so that you don't forget what you need.

STEP SIXTEEN
UNLOADING TRASH

If you had old carpet to remove and haul away, you will have a lot of garbage to unload.

Most carpet stores have a dumpster to use for your trash if the carpet was purchased there. If not you will need to make a trip to the dump .

After the garbage has been removed from the van, **give the van a good sweeping out and make sure everything is orderly.**

RECYCLING

Carpet pad can be recycled if your area has a recycling policy. Keep the pad separated from the other trash, so that it can be taken in for recycling.

QUIZ - TRIMMING AND TUCK-ING - Part one

1. To trim the carpet shorter you turn the handle of the trimmer?
      (a) Towards the wall.
      (b) Keep it straight up and down.
      (c) Away from the wall.
      (d) You never want to trim carpet shorter

2. Carpet should always be trimmed?
    (a) To the same length for all jobs.
    (b) Longer if there is more space under the baseboards.
    (c) Longer if the baseboards are flat on the floor.
    (d) By your boss

3. If you trim the carpet too short?
    (a) You will have to buy all new carpet.
    (b) You will never cut the carpet too short.
    (c) You can stretch it up a little closer with the power stretcher.
    (d) b & c

4. When tucking the carpet?
    (a) Make sure there is a smooth crease.
    (b) Leave any loose strings sticking up.
    (c) Don't worry if the carpet comes loose of the tack strip.
    (d) None of the above

5. Baseboards that are installed with a low rounded type of quarter round......
    a) are excellent for carpet installation
    (b) have a tendency to cause the carpet to come untucked
    (c) should be removed prior to installation
    (d) both b and c

6. **T/F Start with the trimmer handle straight up and down** and if it needs to be trimmed shorter or longer adjust your trimming by turning the handle farther in or out.

7. **T/F You tuck the carpet by pulling up on the cut edge of the carpet** using a tucker. This pulls the carpet out of the gully. (The space between the wall and the tack strip.)

8. **T/F You trim the carpet into a pin metal** by holding the edge of the carpet tightly against the metal with one hand and top cutting through the carpet. Use the outer edge of the metal lip as a guide to run your knife along.

9. **T/F Floor registers are cut from the bottom of the carpet by slicing an X in the center**, then cutting around the edges with a wall trimmer.

QUIZ - PICKING UP
Part two

1. When leaving a job you should?
    (a) Hurry very fast because you want to get home.
    (b) Walk through a final time to make sure nothing was forgotten.
    (c) Throw the tool boxes any place in the van so you can leave faster.
    (d) Ask for a soda since you did a good job.

2. During snow and rain you will want to?
    (a) Lay a scrap of pad or carpet by the doorway.
    (b) Take the day off.
    (c) Not worry about tracking in be cause its not your house anyway.
    (d) Both b and c.

3. As you are working and finish with a tool...
    (a) set them on a counter
    (b) set them back near the tool boxes
    (c) set them on the window sill
    (d) carry them back to the van

Answers Part One
1. A 2. B 3. C 4. A 5. D 6. T 7. F 8. T 9. F

Answers Part Two
1. B 2. A 3. B

SECTION 3
GLUE DOWN CARPET
INSTALLATION

Art Work: © 2002 Eric M. Larson

Glue down carpet installations are more common in commercial applications than in residential, but are used in both residential and commercial situations.

Direct glued down installations are often used in large commercial jobs such as office buildings. Also a lot of sun porches, screened porches, entry ways and kitchens are glued down. Glued down carpet holds up very well in high traffic areas and areas that get a lot of moisture.

Direct glued down carpet is excellent for many areas such as kitchens and baths where a lot of spills are made. Most outdoor carpet installations are glued direct.

REASONS FOR USING A GLUE DOWN INSTALLATION

⇒ THE AREA IS TO LARGE TO POWER STRETCH

⇒ IT IS A VERY HIGH TRAFFIC AREA

⇒ THE AREA IS SUBJECT TO A LOT OF MOISTURE

⇒ CHAIRS AND CARTS WILL BE ROLLED ON THE AREA HEAVILY

⇒ THE COST OF PADDING WOULD BE OVER BUDGET

⇒ TACK STRIP CAN NOT BE ATTACHED TO THE TYPE OF FLOOR

TYPES OF GLUE DOWN INSTALLATIONS

There are three main types of glue down carpet installations. These are the **full spread direct glue installation**, the **double glue installation**, and the **perimeter glue installation**.

For a full spread direct glue installation the entire floor is spread with an adhesive using a trowel. This is the most common glue down installation and we will focus on this type of installation.

For a **double glue installation** a specialized pad for double glue is glued to the floor using a full spread application. Then the carpet is glued direct to the pad using a full spread application. This would be used where padding is to be installed, but the area is to large to power stretch in. Or if tack strip can not be attached to the floor.

For a **perimeter glue installation** only the perimeter of the room and seams are glued. This method is **only used with a non - wrinklable type of carpet**. (See section 6 non - stretchable carpets.)

Directly gluing down carpet is quick, because you don't stretch the carpet, and no pad or tack strip is installed prior to installing. The seams are placed directly together into the adhesive, so it is not necessary to waiting for the seams to cool.

STEP ONE
CLEANLINESS OF THE FLOOR

The floor needs to be very clean of dust and debris for glue down carpet. There is not any pad to hide bumps caused from anything that could be left under the carpet. Such as chips of wood or irregularities in the floor such as cracks

One side of the room carpet is folded back to begin glueing. Pour a pile of adhesive on the floor, then spread along the edges first before starting to spread the center. Once the edges are glued spread with a sweeping motion.

Spread the entire floor evenly, and do not leave any globs of glue behind.

and unevenness.

The floor must be dry and clean of any oil or grease, it also must be clean of dust and dirt. Dust can ball up in the glue and prevent the carpet from sticking well. Especially make sure the corners and edges are swept out thoroughly. Give the floor a good sweeping or vacuum.

Installation over excessively rough surfaces such as brick, tiles or very rough crumbling concrete is not recommended. The rough surface will show through the carpet on a direct glue installation.

Some **floor prep work may also need to be done** so that the floor is smooth: Such as patching cracks and leveling uneven floor seams. If the areas previously had carpet stretched in all of the tack strip will need to be pulled up.

The room temperature should never fall below 50° degrees anytime. The glue will not cure properly in excessively cold temperatures. The installation temperature should be between 65° - 95° and maintained for at least 72 hours.

GLUE DOWN TEAR UP

The two types of carpet to consider when removing direct glue carpet, are those with pad attached and those with out. Those without pad attached tend to be much less work.

If a Kanga back carpet with foam backing attached was glued direct, than the pad will have to be scraped off with a scraper. For a large job there is a power scraping machine that can be used.

To remove a glue down carpet you start in a corner along the wall. The corners tend to be stuck less firmly. Once you have a corner pulled up, keep pulling. Cut through the top of the carpet in three foot wide strips. The carpet will be easier to pull up in strips than trying to pull up every thing in one piece.

It can be difficult to grip the direct glued carpet with your hands if the adhesive is still gripping tight. Their is a tool made by Crain called carpet clamps that grip the carpet so that you can pull with a handle and achieve a better grip.

After removing the carpet sweep or vacuum the floor to remove any remaining pad and dust. Make sure the steps are clean of any dirt and debris too before starting.

FLOOR SCRAPPING

The floor may need to be scrapped to remove the old glue left on the floor after carpet removal. This gives a smoother surface to glue to and it saves adhesive because a rough surface will use more adhesive. Scrape off any dried joint compound, on new construction sites this will leave a hump on the floor if it is not removed. Any other substances that are stuck to the floor that could leave a hump under the carpet must be removed.

Kanga Back carpet that has been glued direct will leave the pad stuck to the floor and you will have to scrape it off. Kanga Back carpet has the pad attached directly to its backing, and when you pull it up only the top pulls up, leaving the pad stuck to the floor. Use a razor blade scraper to scrape it off, not the short handled type but the type with a four foot handle. A tool like an ice scraper can also be used for scraping up pad.

Another situation that will leave pad stuck to the floor is the double glue installation, in this installation the pad is glued down first, and then the carpet is glued down on top of

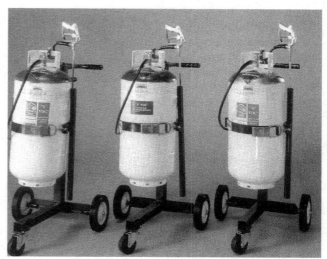

picture are pressurized glue tanks used to spray adhesive on the floor.

Half of one side of the room is spread with adhesive. Spread along the edges, then work your way down the center of the room. Make a straight line with the adhesive along the fold of the carpet. Then it will be easier to glue the other side.

One side of the room is spread with adhesive, now let the adhesive become tacky before folding the carpet back into the adhesive. Clean off the trowel between spreads, to keep it from gumming up.

the pad. It is most common on large commercial jobs. If you get into a large amount of pad to scrape up there is a floor scraping machine that can be rented from a floor covering supply store.

STEP TWO
INSTALLING METALS

The metals used for glue down carpets are pinless metals. You don't need the pins because the carpet isn't stretched. Pin metals are used for stretch-in carpets. The pins are like the pins in tack strip and hold the stretch of the carpet.

Measure the doorway directly under the door hinges and cut the metals to the width needed. Cut all of the metals needed using aviation snips. On a wood floor, nail using ring shank nails or any nail with good holding strength. On a concrete floor, the metals are drilled and then nailed using aluminum nails or masonry nails.

For glue down carpet, in some situations a flat bar metal is used. Flat bars are only used when a pinless metal will not work, such as an uneven transition in the floor. Install the flat bar metals directly over the transition. Nails are put through the top of the metal. On concrete, holes must be pre drilled and plastic anchors set in the hole so that you can nail a flat metal down.

STEP THREE
LAYING OUT THE CARPET

After cleaning and scrapping, doing any floor patching the floor, and installing the metals needed you are ready to carry in the carpet.

The difference between laying out carpet for glue down installation vs stretch in, is that since you are not stretching the carpet all of the relief cuts can be made. But only after you are *sure* that the carpet is in the proper position. The relief cuts allow the carpet to lay down around any corners. Never make any cuts until you are *sure* its laid in exactly the right position.

If there is a straight wall, you can butt the side of the carpet right against the wall to save yourself trimming one wall.

SEAMS FOR DIRECT GLUE INSTAL-LATIONS

If the room is wider than the width of carpet then seams will need to be made. **For a direct glue carpet the seams are glued directly together without seam tape.**

Hot melt seam tape is only used for stretch in carpet, and double glue installations.

Cut all of the seam pieces and lay them in place checking for a good fit. Cut them using a row cutter or a straight edge. Cross seams are normally cut using a square. Make sure every thing is fitting well before you start to glue.

I usually glue down the opposite side of the room in which the seam will be placed first. This will hold the carpet in position, so for the critical seam area it will not shift out of place.

STEP FOUR
FOLDING BACK THE CARPET

Once the carpet is laid out where you want it place some glue buckets and tool boxes on one side for weight to keep the carpet from shifting out of place while it's being pulled back to spread the glue. Allow 3 extra inches of carpet up each wall as you would for stretch-in carpet.

The room is glued down one side at a time. Fold back the carpet so that half of the room can be glued and then the other side. Fold each corner back first so that the carpet doesn't scrape against the wall.

Normally the carpet is folded back so that you have the longest length and narrowest width for gluing, but it can be done either way. It takes a little practice to learn to spread glue proficiently.

STEP FIVE
SPREADING THE GLUE

Pour out enough adhesive to spread with the trowel, but not so much that you can't control it.

Spread along the walls first, being careful not get glue on the walls, then spread in the

TROWEL NOTCH SIZES & ADHESIVE SPREAD

Selecting the correct trowel for the job you are doing, and the carpet you are using: A rough concrete surface will leave more adhesive on the floor so use a smaller notched trowel. A rougher carpet backing will require more adhesive for contact than a smooth backed carpet. Adjust your trowel notch size for these varying conditions.

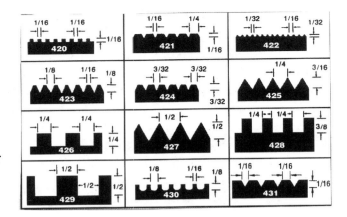

FOR ACTION BACKED CARPETS

1/8th x 1/8th x 1/8th U notched trowel
10 yards per gallon

3/32 x 3/32 x 3/32 V notched trowel
13 yards per gallon

FOR KANGA BACKED & ENHANCER BACKED

1/8th x 1/8th x 1/8th U notched trowel
10 yards per gallon

3/32 x 3/32 x 3/32 V notched trowel
13 yards per gallon

FOR A DOUBLE GLUE - Between the floor and the pad

I recommend a release adhesive to be used between the floor and the pad, this will allow the pad to be pulled loose of the floor when the carpet is being replaced.

1/16th x 1/16th x 1/16th square notch trowel
20 yards per gallon

FOR A DOUBLE GLUE - Between pad and the carpet

1/8th x 1/8th x 1/16th U notch trowel
5 yards per gallon

FOR UNITARY OR WOVEN CARPETS

1/8th x 1/8th x 1/16th U notch trowel
5 yards per gallon

FOR OUTDOOR INSTALLATIONS

1/8th x 1/8th x 1/8th U notched trowel
10 yards per gallon

3/32 x 3/32 x 3/32 V notched trowel
13 yards per gallon

Pictured is a stand up trowel, this saves your knees and back, making the work easier.

center using a sweeping side to side motion.

There are several products that have been developed as alternatives to trowels. The first is a jet sprayer and the other a type of trowel that you use standing up instead of on your knees.

If you are doing a lot of large glue down jobs, **you may want to purchase an adhesive jet sprayer**. Its up to 60% faster than using a trowel. The adhesive is in pressurized tanks and it's sprayed on using a spray nozzle standing on your feet.

Glue is spread evenly across the floor using a trowel. Make sure you don't leave any lumps of glue behind. Pour out a pile of glue, and begin spreading it evenly across the floor, using a side to side sweeping motion. **Make sure not to glue yourself into a corner.**

It also takes time for your hands to become strong enough so you don't become tired but you will get used to it.

Once the side of the floor you are gluing is completely covered with glue, **allow the adhesive open time**. Let the adhesive become tacky so that when you place your finger into it, it will make strings.

While you are waiting, clean off the excess glue from the trowel by wiping it into the bucket and scraping the trowel onto the back of the carpet. You can use scraps of carpet to clean the trowel.

Set the glue bucket on a scrap of carpet so that you don't spill any glue on the top of the carpet. Then, you can lay the carpet back into the glued area.

ROLLING THE CARPET

A heavy carpet roller normally 50 - 75lbs is used to press the carpet into the glue to get a good adhesive transfer. All direct-glue carpets should be rolled with a roller for the correct bond.

Start rolling in the center and work your way outward systematically working any bubbles out of the carpet. For areas to small to use a stand up roller on, you can use a hand roller.

A substitute for a roller is your tool box tray. For small areas some installers use this method but, you will not know if you are using the correct weight. None the less it will work for small areas. Grip the handle and place all of your upper body weight on the tray sliding it across the carpet.

Adhesive transfer means that the floor is completely covered with adhesive and the backing of the carpet is completely covered. This is the proper amount of adhesive transfer from the floor to the carpet backing.

DIRECT GLUE SEAMING

Lay one side of the carpet into the adhesive. Then use a seam seal on the edge that is laid in to be seamed. It is only applied to the one side of the carpet.

Direct glue seam sealer is a contact cement type of seam sealer. This is applied with an adhesive applicator bottle. Apply a small bead just on the cut edge of the carpet.

Put the seam pieces directly into the glue and nudge together with the carpet that is already in the glue. Use the knee kicker to push the seam

A carpet roller is used to roll the carpet into the adhesive for a good adhesive transfer.

together tight.

GLUE DOWN CAUTIONS

Use a carpet scrap to set your trowels and open glue buckets on. Be cautious not to spill any adhesive on top of the carpet, but if you do latex based adhesives will clean up with water while it is fresh.

Any glue that has spilled on the carpet or gotten on the walls can be cleaned off using a thinner cleaning solution. First try water for cleaning any spills, if that doesn't work then use a thinner cleaner. If its dried or is an outdoor adhesive, a cleaner solvent is used.

TYPES OF ADHESIVE

Latex adhesive is the most common type of carpet adhesive as it is a multipurpose carpet adhesive. Latex adhesives are normally indoor adhesives unless they are formulated for outdoor use.

All weather adhesives are normally a **solvent based adhesive**. They are water resistant for outside weather conditions.

Release adhesive is used between the floor and pad on a double glue installation, I would also recommend this adhesive for use with a kanga back carpet installation.

Seam seal adhesives are formulated of latex, for use with hot melt seaming. Solvent based seam seal adhesives are for glue down carpets.

Adhesives should be conditioned for use at a temperature of between 65% - 95%

CLEANING THE TROWEL

Clean the towel after every use. I also wipe off the trowel between glue spreading. Cut pieces of carpet scraps to clean off your trowel. I don't use water to avoid the trowel from rusting.

The slight amount of glue that dries on the trowel can be scraped off with a scrapper before the next use.

STEP SIX
TRIMMING GLUE DOWN CARPET

To trim glued down carpet take a tucker, I use a vinyl knife as a tucker, and press the carpet into the corner. Create a crease along the walls by scraping with the tucker, and pressing the carpet into the glue, and into the corner.

A good crease ensures that the carpet will be trimmed well. If it is not pressed into the corner tightly and you try to trim it you will not have an even trim. Once a good crease is created then cut directly on it with a carpet knife.

If you trim the carpet too short you can nudge it closer to the wall with the knee kicker.

There is a trimmer that is designed for glue down carpets, but many installers simply cut using a carpet knife as described. If you are doing a lot of glue down jobs a specific trimmer for this would be a good investment.

A trimmer used for glue down carpet looks like the one used to trim stretch in carpet, but it cuts the carpet net (exact) to the wall, where a regular trimmer cuts the carpet longer for stretch in installations. The carpet fits perfectly to the wall with no excess.

DOUBLE GLUE INSTALLATIONS

For a **double glue installation,** a specialized pad for double glue is glued to the floor using a full spread application, and preferably a release adhesive. The carpet is glued direct to the pad using a full spread application. Use a premium stick adhesive, you want the carpet to be bonded to the pad very well.

This type of installation would be used where padding is to be installed, but the area is to large too power stretch in. Or if tack strip can not be attached to the floor, but padding is still needed.

Seams for a double glue installation are seamed using hot melt seam tape. The seam tape is place under the seam area. Latex the cut edges for the seam with seam seal latex.

Roll a double glue installation with a roller weighing 50 lb. - 35 lb. or use a stiff broom.

INSTALLING GLUE-DOWN STEPS

Measure the width of the step and cut the carpet for the steps. Plush carpets are usually cut from the back for steps, using the straight edge. Berber carpet is most always row cut.

Lay the carpet in place on the steps to check for the proper fit. You also are checking to see how many steps the piece will cover, so you can start gluing on that step. Remove all of the carpet from the steps, laying it at the bottom of the steps on the floor.

Start gluing with the top step that the carpet is to cover, and pour a small amount of adhesive on it. Using the trowel spread the glue evenly on the foot of each step, coming down the steps. Also glue the riser of the step.

Once all of the steps are glued, press the carpet into place, starting from the bottom step. Use the stair tool to hammer a crease in the center of the foot and the riser, making a good crease. Continue this up all of the steps.

Many installers staple into the corner of the foot and riser on direct glue steps, then use the stair tool to make a crease. This will also set in any staples that are showing. This holds the carpet in place for the adhesive to dry, but also can show staple marks. To avoid using staples and and staple marks, you let the adhesive set up to hold the carpet in place on the step before moving on.

OUTDOOR DIRECT GLUE

Carpet is installed outdoors in many situations, porches, swimming pools, boats, and steps are some of these areas.

An outdoor carpet, that is made for outdoors, must be used for outdoor installations.

Select an outdoor adhesive that is designed for outdoor use.

QUIZ - SECTION 3
DIRECT GLUE INSTALLATION

1. When gluing down carpet, the floor. . .
   (a) Needs to be clean of dust and debris so it does not ball up in the glue.
   (b) Doesn't have to be clean.
   (c) Should be very cold.
   (d) Should be slightly damp.

2. The metals for glue down carpet are. . .
   (a) The same as for stretch-in carpet.
   (b) Are pinless metals.
   (c) In 10' long strips.
   (d) Both b and c.
   (e) none of the above.

3. When spreading glue do not leave behind any. . .
   (a) Lumps of glue.
   (b) Pieces of wood.
   (c) Both a & b.
   (d) adhesive.

4. You use a _____ to spread glue?
   (a) Trowel.
   (b) Spreader.
   (c) Trimmer.
   (d) all of the above.

5 To achieve a good cut when trimming a glue down installation using a carpet knife you make.....
   (a) a relief cut.
   (b) a good crease in the corner.
   (c) a new type of hand trimmer.
   (d) both a and b.

Answers
1. A   2. B   3. C   4. A   5. B

A finished flight of wrap around steps

SECTION 4
CARPETING STEPS

Art Work: © 2002 Eric M. Larson

BASICS OF STEP INSTALLATION

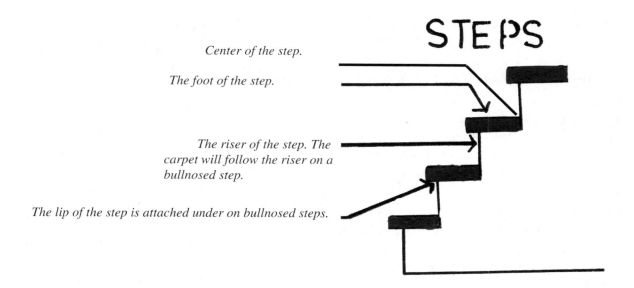

Center of the step.

The foot of the step.

The riser of the step. The carpet will follow the riser on a bullnosed step.

The lip of the step is attached under on bullnosed steps.

◊ REMOVE OLD FLOOR COVERING FROM THE STEPS

◊ MEASURE THE WIDTH OF THE STEPS

◊ CUT THE TACK STRIP 1 INCH NARROWER THAN THIS MEASUREMENT

◊ INSTALL TACK STRIP ON THE FOOT AND THE RISER OF EACH STEP

◊ USE THE WIDTH OF THE HAMMER HEAD TO PLACE TACK STRIP AWAY FROM THE CENTER

◊ ENSURE THAT EACH END ON THE TACK STRIP HAS A NAIL

◊ FACE THE PINS IN TOWARDS THE CENTER OF THE STEP

◊ CUT THE PAD IN 6 FOOT STRIPS TO THE WIDTH OF THE STEP

◊ STAPLE PAD ON THE STEP WITH A HAMMER STAPLER

◊ TRIM PAD TO THE LENGTH OF THE STEP NEXT TO THE TACK STRIP

◊ CUT THE CARPET TO THE WIDTH OF THE STEP

◊ THE NAP (pile) OF THE CARPET RUNS DOWN THE STEP

◊ KNEE KICK THE CARPET TO HOOK IT ON TO THE TACK STRIP AND TIGHTEN THE CARPET

◊ HAMMER THE CARPET INTO EACH CENTER OF THE STEP WITH A STAIR TOOL

Their are many types of steps and I will go into most of these variations later in this section.

For now, I will go into detail as how to install a basic **Waterfall step, with walls on both sides.** I will explain in detail installing tack strip, pad, cutting the carpet and kicking the carpet on to the step in the waterfall fashion.

Waterfall steps, with walls on both sides, are the most basic of steps to install. The one variation you can make, if you prefer this look, is to bullnose the step.

To **Bullnose a step** you staple (or attach with adhesive) the carpet under the lip on the riser, so that rather than having the carpet flow over the riser it is tight against it.

Pictured is a flight of steps with tack strip installed properly on the riser and foot of each step.

STEP ONE
REMOVING OLD CARPET & PAD FROM STEPS

To remove the old carpet and pad from the steps, you should determine how the old carpet was installed. It may have been installed using tack strip as is recommended for stretch-in carpet. This is the easiest for removal. Grip the carpet at the bottom of the step with pliers and start pulling. It is not stapled or glued on in this case.

If the carpet was stapled onto the step, use the same method only be careful not to cut your hands on staples. (Stapling steps on is not recomended!)

Padding is simply pulled off with your hands. Use the bottom of your shoe to remove any pieces of pad stuck to the staples. Remove with pliers or hammer down any staples that are sticking up.

STEP TWO
INSTALLING TACK STRIP ON STEPS WITH WALLS ON BOTH SIDES

If tack strip is not already installed on the steps it will need to be installed to stretch the carpet on properly.

Tack strip is installed on the riser and the foot of the step with the pins facing in towards each other to hold the carpet on after knee kicking it. The carpet will be hammered into the joint in the center of the step, between the two pieces of tack strip, using a stair tool and a hammer. This keeps the carpet held in place and creates a straight line (crease).

If the steps already have tack strip installed, inspect the strips to make sure that they are all nailed on securely, give them a pull if they look like they might not be secured. Check the ends of each piece of strip to make sure they have nails in them. Add nails to any that are not nailed adequately. Check that they are not rotting, with the pins rusting off, or not installed the correct distance apart.

Make sure that the foot and the riser both have tack strip installed. Sometimes only the foot was installed with tack strip, this is not correct for stretching on carpet. When using this method you would have to staple into the corner of each step in order to hold the carpet on. Using excess staples is not recommended, they often show and this is why tack strip is preferred. Installing tack strip only to the foot, and not the riser of the step is done in order to save money, by not using as much tack strip.

The tack strip is installed back further on steps than in a room next to walls. Install it 1 and 1/8th of an inch from where the riser and the step meet. (Or the thickness of the hammer head, if it is this thickness). Tack strip is installed both on the riser of the step and the foot or tread (the area that you walk on.) If the tack strip is installed to close too the center it will be very difficult to kick the carpet on and have it hold onto the pins. It also will be difficult to hammer the carpet into the center using the stair tool to make a good crease.

First count the number of steps to determine how many pieces of tack strip you will need. For a normal flight of twelve steps it would take 24 pieces, one piece for each foot, and one for each riser. The tack strip comes in four foot long pieces and most steps are less than 3 feet wide. This will leave you a lot of small pieces left over. I always cut 3 or 4 less pieces than I need of tack strip, and use the small left overs to do the rest of the foot area of the steps. Lay out all of the new 4 foot tack strip you will need in a pile on the floor.

Then measure the width of each step to the nearest 1/8th of an inch. Measure every other step to acquire an average width. The tack strip

can be cut one inch narrower than the steps so that they fit easily. This allows a half inch on each side for extra space. Steps don't always run straight and can vary in width by up to an inch. Lay the tape measure out across the floor, to measure the new tack strips. Cut all of the pieces that you need to the average width of the steps. Once you have cut the first piece of tack strip it is not necessary to measure every single one with the tape measure. You can estimate where to cut on the tack strip by the nails in the tack strip.

The risers are installed first. Pick up the cut pieces of tack strip that are needed for the risers and lay one piece of strip on each step. Position them with the pins facing in toward the center, (the pins will face down towards the foot of the step on the riser pieces.)

Start with the top step for installing tack strip on the riser and work your way down the steps. Sit on the top landing and lean over. Install

The pad is installed on steps. For waterfall steps the pad is installed over the riser, as shown. For a bullnosed step the pad is only installed on the foot of each step.

STEPS

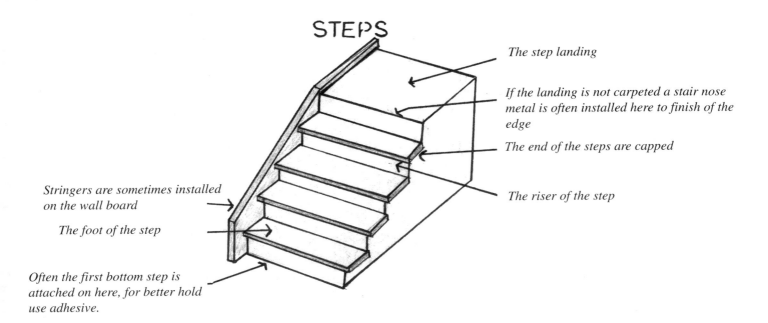

The step landing

If the landing is not carpeted a stair nose metal is often installed here to finish of the edge

The end of the steps are capped

The riser of the step

Stringers are sometimes installed on the wall board

The foot of the step

Often the first bottom step is attached on here, for better hold use adhesive.

each piece the width of the hammer head from the center of the step. The pins face down toward the foot of the step. Use an extra nail on any ends that are missing nails. Work your way down each step to the bottom. The bottom riser of the first step is not always installed with tack strip. It is often necessary to staple (or use a glue gun) to attach the carpet on the bottom of the first step, because the carpet does not seem to hold as well to the first bottom riser.

Next, install the tack strip on the foot (tread) of each step. Lay one piece of strip on each step, then use all the small left over pieces. Face the pins in towards the riser. Estimate the distance of the strip from the center to be a hammer head width away. Start at the bottom of the steps and work your way up when installing tack strip on the foot of the step. Nail any ends that don't have nails.

After installing the tack strip properly, then install the pad.

STEP THREE
INSTALLING PAD ON STEP

Carpet padding comes in 6 foot wide rolls. Cut the padding to the width of the steps using a 6 foot straight edge. For example you might cut them to the width of 39 inches x 6' width of the pad.

Start installing pad on the top step and staple the pad to the foot of the step near the tack strip. Then, wrap the pad over the riser and staple the pad above the tack strip on the riser. Cut the pad off above the tack strip on the riser. Continue this all the way down the steps.

A hammer stapler is used to attach the pad on steps. Keep a box of pad staples nearby so that you don't have to run to get them every time you run out of staples. You will be using a lot of staples to install the pad.

Measuring to cut the carpet for the steps. A straight edge is used to guide the edge. Measure and mark on the backing with a pencil if you like. Cut the carpet very accurately. (It must be exactly the right width.)

Pictured they are putting the carpet into place on the steps to test for a proper fit.

STEP FOUR
CUTTING AND INSTALLING CARPET ON STEPS

Measure the width of the steps very closely before cutting the carpet for the steps. Measure every other step to determine if they are all the same width. Usually the carpet can be cut at a slight angle to allow for steps running narrower or wider in width. If every step is a completely different width than you would have to cut and install each step separately. Hopefully they all run straight.

Cut plush carpet from the back using a 6

foot straight edge. If you cut it too narrow then you will have a gap along the edge. If you cut the carpet to wide, it will bow from being too tight.

Berber and level loop carpets are always cut with a row cutter rather than a straight edge.

Be certain to measure the carpet accurately so that it fits perfectly on each step. I often use a pencil and make several marks on the backing for the first cuts. Be very careful that the straight edge doesn't move as you are cutting. As I cut the carpet I keep my knee held on the bottom of

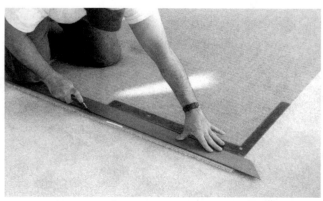

Using a square and straight edge to square the starting end of the botton step.

Picture-pushing carpet into each step making sure they fit just right.

Pictured, the knee kicker is kicked and the carpet stretched onto the steps.

the straight edge and hold the top tightly with my hand.

Carpet should fit flush on the starting riser on the bottom stair. Cut the bottom of the step carpet using a square and straight edge so that it starts square on the first riser.

Test the carpet that you cut by laying it on the steps to be sure it fits correctly. The nap (pile) direction always runs down the steps. Continue to push the carpet down into each step to check for the proper fit. If the carpet is not fitting properly remove it and cut off any excess.

Once it is determined that the carpet fits into each step without binding or leaving a gap along the wall then they are ready to install.

Most installers don't wear knee pads when kicking on steps because they feel that they get in the way. I have always worn knee pads even when kicking on steps. Kick with the lower part of your thigh and not directly with your knee cap area.

You use the knee kicker to stretch the steps carpet on, and hook it to the tack strip. Keep the head of the knee kicker just behind the tack strip. Hold down tight on the knee kicker, so that it grips well into the carpet. Next, swing back with your knee and kick. Do this all of the way across the step until it is tight.

Use a hammer and stair tool to hammer the carpet between the tack strip after stretching it on. This wedges the carpet between the two pieces of tack strip on the foot and riser and secures the carpet onto the tack strip. Stair tooling the carpet will make a crease in the center of the steps. (This ensures that the carpet won't come loose and it looks good.)

SOME OTHER TYPES OF STEPS

In addition to the basic **waterfall steps with walls on both sides** described above, there are: pie steps, round steps, steps with capped ends and spindles, bird cage steps, and step runners.

These steps can all be installed as a **waterfall step**, where the carpet flows straight down the riser, like a waterfall. Or, as a variation they can be bullnosed. **Bullnosing a step** involves attaching the carpet under the lip on the riser.

Pictured hammering the stair tool into the center of each step. It is used to pound the carpet into the center of the tack strip to hold well and create a smooth crease.

Pictured are steps with spindles and capped ends prior to carpeting. Each step needs to be installed one step at a time. Cut the carpet to go through the spindles and then kick the step on. Once the step is kicked on then cap the ends.

You will come across many different situations when installing steps such as ledges, spindles, various types of upholstery work, and on and on...

STEPS WITH CAPPED ENDS AND SPINDLES

These can be installed in a waterfall fashion, or bullnosed. The capped steps pictured are installed in a waterfall fashion.

The method used to cap the ends and install around the spindles is the most critical factor in a quality looking capped end. Install tack strip all around the spindles, so that the carpet can be tucked around the spindles. The seam is placed between the spindles and not over the capped end. Use hot melt glue to hold the carpet.

Hold the carpet over the capped end and place two cut marks where it should be cut. After cutting to fit, you staple the carpet under the capped end. The corners and rolled riser carpet are attached using a hot melt glue gun.

This is a finished flight of steps with capped ends and spindles. These steps were not bull-nosed. Upholstered steps tend to be more difficult to install using a Berber carpet as shown. Steps with capped ends and spindales are some of the most difficult steps to carpet.

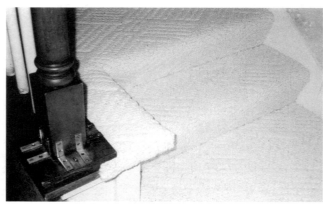

Pictured is a ledge that is upholstered.

Pictured installing the riser on a round step. On a round step like this the top piece is installed first and bull-nosed. Next the bottom is wrapped around it and stapled on.

Pictured are steps and a landing with pad and tack strip installed. They are ready to be carpeted. The corner of the first top step is going to be capped. Their is no pad installed on the corner that will be capped.

Round steps are not as difficult to install as they look. Pictured is the finsished round step installed with berber carpet.

Pictured is the finished step. It has a capped end and is done with berber carpet. Note that the steps are waterfalled but the capped end of the step is bullnosed. (The steps themselves were not bullnosed.)

Pictured is a flight of pie-steps that are bull-nosed (stapled under the lip.) Bullnosed steps can be done with out staples by using adhesive on the riser of the step. They are called pie steps because they are shaped like slices of pie.

PIE STEPS

Pie steps are as the name implies, shaped like pieces of a pie. Pie steps can be installed in a waterfall fashion, or bullnosed. Each pie step needs to be installed individually.

The biggest mistake in installing a pie shaped step is cutting the carpet to small. Measure the largest area in the width and in the length. These steps use a big piece of carpet. Start with a big square piece of carpet that is cut to the largest measurements of the step.

Install the step and then cut off the excess carpet. You can often use the cut off piece for another step.

BIRD CAGE STEPS

This is a bottom step, that forms a circle on one or both sides of the step, a hand rail follows the circle. The hand rail spindles form a circle on the end of the step that looks like a bird cage.

Bird cage steps can be installed in a waterfall fashion or bullnosed. To bullnose this step the riser is installed as a separate piece of carpet. The foot of the step must be cut so that the seam is between the spindles.

To install a birdcage step in a waterfall fashion is more difficult. The round ends of the bird cage step must be hand sewn to install in a waterfall fashion. First, cut the foot of the step to fit around the spindles, than draw a line on the back of the carpet to follow the round end of the step. Cut this so that the carpet flows over the step and fits against the riser. Fit the riser and foot pieces together and draw another line, cut this line.

When you are sure the carpet fits perfectly together you can hand sew it. Turn the carpet inside out to hand sew.

When installing the carpet on the step put contact cement on the pad where the hand sewn seams are, this will keep the seam from spreading apart.

ROUND STEPS

A round step can be installed bullnosed or as a waterfall step. Bullnosing a round step is much easier, because it will have to be hand sewn to install as a waterfall step.

To bullnose you will install the riser as a separate piece of carpet, and install the top of the step separately.

To install a round step in a waterfall fashion, the top and riser will have to be hand sewn together.

When installing the finished sewn piece, use contact cement on the pad of the hand sewn area. This will keep the seam pulled in tight and keep it from opening up.

BULLNOSING STEPS

A bullnosed step follows straight up the riser of the step, and wraps around the lip of the step. The same step installed in a water fall fashion flows over the riser like a waterfall would.

A bullnosed step has a tailored look that some feel is a fancier look, this is a matter of personal opinion. Bullnosed steps do take more time to install.

Install the tack strip on the foot of the step and the riser as usual. Some installers prefer not to install the tack strip on the riser for bullnosed steps so that the carpet looks very flat on the riser. The pad is installed only on the foot and just over the lip. Duck tape the pad where it wraps over for added protection, to keep it from tearing and wearing.

To attach the carpet under the lip of the step most installers staple it up under the lip with a gillie gun stapler. This is the quickest method and the staples usually do not show under the lip. Other installers prefer to use a spray adhesive on the riser to attach it for a bullnosed step. This is more time consuming but you will not have any chance of staples showing.

STRINGERS

Stringers are the carpeting installed on the wall boards of the steps. They are put on in long strips. Install the stringers first (Prior to installing the steps) so that the step carpet covers your cuts.

Attach the top of the stringers with adhesive. The bottom cuts are covered when the step carpet is installed, so this area can be stapled on.

You will be doing a lot of top cutting on stringers and this dulls your knife blades very fast. Keep plenty of blades in your knife storage compartment. Change blades frequently to make the cutting easier and give a smoother cut.

RUNNERS ON STEPS

A runner is carpet installed only in the center of the step, leaving the sides wood. Runners are also installed in hallways. The carpet edges on the sides is preferably bound, or surged. It is possible to roll the carpet edge but is very time consuming, and may not be possible with a very stiff carpet.

Measure in on the sides and mark with a pencil. You will need this to keep the runner installed straight on the step.

Install tack strip leaving an inch of space on each side, keeping the strip within the lines drawn. Install pad on the step, also keep this in one inch on each side, to the same width as the tack strip.

The carpet is kicked on as you would a

Pictured installing the stringers on the wall boards of the step. Installing stringers is time consuming. Strips of carpet are cut and hot melt glued to the top of the runner. Then they are each cut individually and stapled on close to the riser and foot. (Remember to staple between the nap of the carpet so that the staples do not show.) The stringers are installed prior to the pad and carpet, this allows the carpet to cover the cuts and staples for a finished look.

waterfall step, or can also be bullnosed.

WRAP AROUND STEPS (FLOATERS)

Wrap around steps are also known as floaters, the carpet wraps all of the way around these steps. Tack strip is installed on the back of the step. Pad is installed on the foot and preferably over the front lip. Place duct tape over the pad on the lip to protect the pad from wear.

The carpet is attached on the bottom or back lip of the step. Many installers feel that the seam hides better if it is on the back lip of the step rather than on the center of the bottom of the step. The carpet is attached using a gillie gun stapler or with a hot melt glue gun. The glue gun

Here is a finished flight of waterfall steps with stringers on the sides using plush carpet. The top step is finished with a stair nose metal because their is vinyl installed on the landing. If the landing were carpeted their would be no metal.

Pictured is a flight of wrap around steps with two finished and the rest only with pad installed. Pad is installed only on the foot of a wrap around step.

wall are capped.

Capped ends: steps without any wall on *one or both sides of the steps. The ends are wrapped around and stapled underneath, they are cut and upholstered.*

QUIZ - SECTION 4 STEPS

1. Tack strip is installed. . .
    (a) Only on the foot of the step.
    (b) Only along walls.
    (c) Both on the foot and riser of the step.
    (d) None of the above.

2. Pad is attached on the steps using a _____. . .
    (a) Pad glue.
    (b) Hammer stapler.
    (c) Piece of Tack strip.
    (d) Knee kicker.

3. To stretch the carpet on the steps you use a _____. . .
    (a) Knee kicker.
    (b) Power stretcher.
    (c) Hammer Stapler.
    (d) All of the above.

4. Tack strip on steps is installed _____. . .
    (a) The width of a hammer head from the center of the step.
    (b) The thickness of your finger away.
    (c) Both a and b.
    (d) 2 inches.

5. You hammer the carpet into the center to make a crease using a _____.
    (a) Stair Tool.
    (b) Hammer.
    (c) Both a & b.
    (d) None of the above.

6. **T/F** To remove the old carpet and pad from the steps, you should determine how the old carpet was installed. It may have been installed using tack strip as is recommended for

will hide the seam better than staples will. This becomes critical with a carpet that has a dense plush pile because the staples will show.

It requires two people to install wrap around steps. One person under the steps to attach the carpet, and the other on top with the knee kicker.

Measure the distance around the step using a cloth tape measure. Or use a piece of the carpet you are using to measure around the step. Every step will vary slightly in the distance around, so you must measure every step individually and cut each piece of carpet for each step individually. You must have an accurate measurement to cut the carpet the correct size. Cut the piece of carpet slightly smaller to allow for the stretch.

The ends of the steps that are not next to the

stretch-in carpet. This is the most difficult type of removal.

7. **T/F** If tack strip is not already installed on the steps it will not need to be installed to stretch the carpet on properly, just use a stapler.

8. **T/F The tack strip is installed back further on steps than they are in a room next to walls.** Install it 1 and 1/8th of an inch from where the riser and the step meet.

9. **T/F** Start installing pad on the top step and staple the pad to the foot of the step near the tack strip. Then, wrap the pad over the riser and staple the pad above the tack strip on the riser. Cut the pad off above the tack strip on the riser. Continue this all the way down the steps.

10. **T/F** Test the carpet that you cut by laying it on the steps to be sure it fits correctly. The nap (pile) direction always runs sideways on the steps.

11. **T/F** Bird cage steps can be installed in a waterfall fashion or bullnosed. To bullnose the step the riser is installed as a separate piece of carpet.

12. **T/F** A bullnosed step follows straight up the riser of the step, and wraps around the lip of the step. The same step installed in a water fall fashion flows over the riser like a waterfall would.

13. **T/F** For a wrap around step, the carpet wraps all of the way around the steps and is seamed together on the top of the step.

14. **T/F** A runner is carpet installed only in the center of the step, leaving the sides wood. Runners are also installed in hallways.

Answers
1. C 2. B 3. A 4. A 5. C 6. F 7. F
8. T 9. T 10. F 11. T 12.T 13. F 14. T

SECTION 5
SOME OTHER SITUATIONS

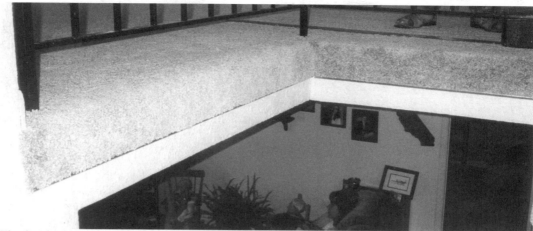

The finished ledge and railing with carpet installed around the posts and in a metal. The seams can not be seen so that the finished ledge looks pleasing when entering the home. This is the first thing everyone coming into the home will see, so extra time and effort must be taken to ensure an excellent looking ledge.

CARPETING OVER A LEDGE WITH A RAILING

Wrapping carpet over ledges with railings to cut and go around has been a huge problem area with installers using carpets with low dense naps (piles). This is a high visibility area. Everyone that walks into the home will see this ledge.

Many homes with wrap ledges were not correctly built to be carpeted unless a shag was used. When these homes were built in the 60's and 70's shag carpet was all the rage. You could roll the edges of these carpets and nail them down without any marks showing. You could make cuts through railings without ever knowing that the carpet was cut. With today's modern carpets more care must be taken.

There are two major problems with these homes:

1. Cutting the carpet to go through the railing can show cut marks very badly in modern carpets.

2. Wrapping the carpet over the ledge and nailing it into dry wall with the carpet edge rolled shows every nail and staple mark.

The first method that can be used to solve these problems is to install a new type of railing. Wood railings are made so that there is a piece of wood on the floor and the carpet can be tucked next to it, instead of wrapping over the ledge. The ledge can be trimmed with finished wood boards.

* The first problem is the railing posts. Cutting around them can show cut marks if not done properly. I know of two methods of installing around railings with posts:

METHOD # 1. Leave the railing in place and install around it. The railing is bolted to the floor; install pad over the plates leaving room to tuck around the post. Glue the pad to the plate using hot melt glue. Carefully cut the carpet to go around the railing. It can be tricky to cut when the carpet is folded back because angles are cut the opposite direction that it first appears.

The carpet is folded back to make the cuts around the railing posts. They are cut at angles inward and placed around the posts. The carpet is seamed back together around with seam tape and a hot melt glue gun.

A ledge with a 2 x 4 piece of wood is attached for the correct installation of a wraped ledge with carpet. Carpet pad can also be wraped over the ledge for a plush feel and look. Install tack strip around the ledge on the floor to hold the room stretch. Attach the carpet under the board with adhesive or staples to hold it over the wall.

This is one way to carpet over a ledge, nail a pin metals into the wall and set the carpet into the metal. The metal only holds the carpet over the wall and does not hold the stretch of the carpet. Tack strip is installed on the floor around the ledge to hold the stretch of the carpet. Many installers also wrap pad over the wall, this gives a plush feel and look.

The carpet is then wraped around the post and placed into the metal. The corner will need to be patched, when wrapping a ledge you are short carpet in the corner. Any carpet that is seamed over a ledge is preferably done by hand sewing to prevent the seam from opening up.

The finished ledge installed over a 2 x 4.

Use seam tape and a glue gun to seam it back together.

METHOD # 2. Remove the railing and when finished installing bolt the railing back over the carpet.

To do this, first remove the railing, and re-screw the bolts back into the floor, leaving them up 1/2 inch so that they can be felt through the carpet. Install the carpet over the top of them. Cut X's to remove the bolts, then reinstall the railing over the top of the carpet. This method will eliminate the cuts around the railing but the plates and bolts will show. Some people may object to the plate and bolts showing but if the plate and bolts are painted it looks pleasing.

You may also make larger X cuts in the carpet around the bolts. This will allow you to bolt the railing back in place under the carpet. When installing the pad leave space for the plates to bolt down. Place seam tape under the carpet splices and seam with a glue gun. This method will eliminate the large cuts around the railing for the smaller ones around the foot of the railing.

* The second problem is attaching the carpet to the ledge so that it does not show staple or dimple marks. I know of two methods of doing this:

METHOD # 1. You can nail a piece of wood to the wall for the carpet to wrap around. The carpet is wrapped around the wood then glued or stapled to the bottom of it. Using a glue gun or contact cement will assure that staples don't show. You do not need an expensive piece of wood. A piece of pine will do. Use a 2 x 4, a 2 x 2, or a 2 x 6 depending on the look you desire. Stapling to the bottom of the board prevents any staple marks, and dimples from showing.

METHOD # 2. A pin metal can be installed on the wall and the carpet installed into it as on a floor. This eliminates installing a board on the wall, and gives a quite pleasing look.

REMOVING CARPET FROM A TRAILER

The original carpet in a trailer home often is turned under and stapled along the walls. Some trailers have the walls built over the top of the carpet.

To remove carpet that is stapled down; grip in a corner along the wall using pliers. Pull the carpet very hard until it's pulling loose. Be careful gripping the carpet because of the long staples sticking out from the back. Grip tightly and pull up all around the edge of the room. Hammer down any staples that are sticking up.

If walls are installed over the top of the carpet use a sharp knife and cut the carpet along the edges of the room, very close to the walls.

CARPETING WALLS

You will be faced with many situations in the carpet profession, and one of those is to carpet walls. I have personally carpeted the walls of entire break rooms. It is also common to carpet the sides of bars.

It is a good idea to have two people working for carpeting walls. You will need help pushing the carpet into the adhesive, and to hold it in place while it is sticking.

Carpet is installed on walls using carpet

An alternative to wrapping carpet over a ledge is to install a new type of railing, that the carpet will tuck up next to.

The railing post by the top step. The carpet is cut and wraped around it, then seamed back together.

Seam the carpet back together around the post. The finished railing post by the top step.

A corner railing post prior to padding. I install pad over the metal and attach it with hot melt glue.

The finished side railing post with carpet installed around it. The seam is next to invisable.

The pad is installied over the railing bolts, and glued down to the metal with hot melt glue, to keep it from puffing up.

adhesive, you can use some staples to hold it in place while the glue is adhering, but not excessively.

Cut the carpet to fit the wall and hold into place to test for fit. Lay the carpet on the floor, ready to push up into the adhesive.

Spread the adhesive onto the wall using a trowel or spray adhesive. Make sure that you have the floor protected, normally the carpet that you will install on the wall is laying backing side up next to the wall and will protect the floor from spills. Have the carpet cut close to size and lying on the floor, but close to the wall that you're installing.

Push the carpet up into place into the glue. You can shift it by pushing with the knee kicker once it is in place. Apply some staples to the top. Use a hand roller and keep rolling the carpet until it sticks into the glue.

To install carpet on the sides of a bar you can cut the carpet to the exact size. Adhesive is applied to the side of the bar. Make sure to lie something on the floor to protect it when using adhesive. Often the carpet you are installing is laid back side up on the floor next to the bar protecting the floor. Wrap the whole piece of carpet around the bar. You may use some staples to hold the carpet in place.

Use the knee kicker and push on it to get the carpet wrapped tight. Roll the wall until the carpet sticks. You may need to staple some to hold the carpet.

I recommend using a 1/8 x1/8 x 1/8th U notch trowel , or a 3/32 x 3/32 x 3/32 V notch trowel for carpeting walls.

A fast tack adhesive is best for carpeting walls, you want the carpet to stick quickly, so you don't have to hold it for a long time.

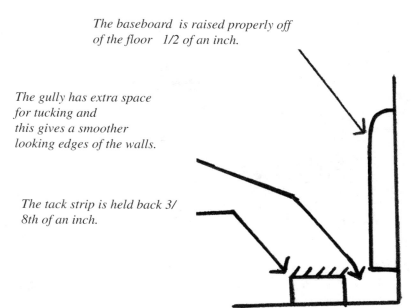

The baseboard is raised properly off of the floor 1/2 of an inch.

The gully has extra space for tucking and this gives a smoother looking edges of the walls.

The tack strip is held back 3/8th of an inch.

Pictured is baseboard properly raised so that the carpet will tuck underneath. Tackstrip is installed 3/8th of an inch back.

CARPETING TOE KICKS

Toe kicks are the riser under kitchen cabinets and bathroom vanities. They are not difficult to carpet and it adds a nice finished touch. The best way to install them is to cut strips of carpet separately to fit perfectly under the toe-kick.

Use the stapler and staple them on, or apply contact cement to glue them on for a stapleless look. They should be installed last after the room is carpeted.

CARPET COVE BASE

Sometimes, in a kitchens, bathroom, or commercial areas, the whole perimeter of the room is cove based with carpet up the lower walls, instead of using vinyl cove base, or wood base boards.

To cove carpet up the walls, nail pinnless metals along the walls approximately 4 inches from the floor. Then cut carpet strips to that width and contact cement or staple them on. Hammer down the metal edge to protect the

#155

A binding machine that is used to bind the edges of carpet for area rugs and carpet cove base. Picture, complements of National Flooring Equipment.

A carpet cove base attachment used to bind carpet cove base. Picture, complements of National Flooring Equipment.

Spray adhesive is used to glue a new backing on custom area rugs. This hides all of the seams used for inlays and borders. Picture, complements of National Flooring Equipment.

Pictured below are borders seamed in area rugs. Borders can be seamed in stretch in wall to wall carpet also. Picture, complements of National Flooring Equipment.

When installing a border the field color is in the center, and the border surrounds the field. The nap (pile) on the border faces in towards the field.

carpet edge.

To cove base walls without metals, the carpet edges are bound or surged instead of using metals. This works best to cove base a large area with carpet cove base, installing the metals would be too time consuming and not cost efficient.

INSTALLING BASE BOARD

When the base board is being installed it should be raised 3/8th - 1/2 inch off of the floor. This allows extra space for the carpet to tuck and makes a smoother edge along the wall. The carpet does not appear to slop down as much along the wall.

For stretch in carpet 1/2 inch is best, the tack strip is 1/2 inch high, including the pins. For direct glue carpet 3/8 of an inch would be best.

Having the base board installed up 3/8th - 1/2 inch makes it easier to trim and gives you a smoother finished edge. The carpet can be trimmed longer and you don't have to trim it as accurately.

Having more carpet tucked under the wall keeps the carpet from stretching away from the wall. When stretching, the carpet can pull slightly away from the wall leaving a gap.

This is primarily when the base boards are flat on the floor not leaving extra space for carpet to tuck. It is even more common for the carpet to stretch away from the wall if quarter round is installed. Watch as you stretch for this situation, you will need to ease off of the power stretcher if you are pulling carpet away from the wall.

You don't always have the perfect conditions and **many times the base board is installed flat on the floor.** This is still not difficult to trim. You just cut the carpet slightly shorter than if the base board were raised up.

BORDERS

A border is when a different carpet is seamed around the perimeter of the room. It can be used for stretch in wall to wall carpet, or be used in making area rugs.

The border carpet is installed with the nap (pile) facing in towards the field carpet. The corners are mitered at 45% angles.

The width of the border depends on the size of the area that you are carpeting, and the look that you want to achieve. A small area such as a hallway or area rug would have a smaller border width, than a large room. Some common border widths are 6", 1', 1'6", 2', and 3'. Use a width that will give you the look you want for the size room you are installing.

The field carpet can be a completely different color and height of carpet than the border. They do not need to be a similar height to look pleasing.

IN LAYS

Patterns are drawn on the back of the carpet and cut out to make designs, lettering, or art work, any thing is possible with an inlay.

The carpet for the inlay is placed on the bottom and the main carpet is on the top. The patterns are cut out from the back. Secure the carpets so they don't move when cutting. A machine is used that cuts through both layers of carpet. You could make two rugs from this of opposite coloring.

Patterns can be made in many ways, pattern paper can be used. There are pattern

A custom inlay installed in a room. The carpet is cut in circles, making a nice custom carpet. Picture, complements of National Flooring Equipment.

A custom inlay carpet installed on steps and a landing. Picture, complements of National Flooring Equipment.

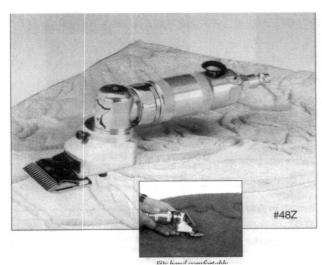

#48Z

A carpet carver is used to carve custom designs in carpet. Below are custom carved carpets. Picture, complements of National Flooring Equipment.

A power cutter is used to cut out custom inlays, it cuts through two layers of carpet. This tool makes cutting inlays very fast and accurate. Picture, complements of National Flooring Equipment.

designs available that are used with an overhead projector to project onto the backing of the carpet. Other tracer projectors are available to enlarge art, photos, designs, and other objects, to trace. Computer software is also available for inlay designs.

A less expensive way of cutting inlays is to make a pattern, and draw it on the backing of your main carpet and the inlay carpet. Use a craft knife, or a hot knife to cut out the inlays.

Inlays are seamed in place from the back of the carpet, and a scrim tape is placed over the seams. This scrim is similar to a drywall scrim. Hot melt glue is used over the scrim to seam the inlays in place. A heavy duty commercial glue gun is used for this. Use a T nozzle to spread a wide area with glue.

Inlays can be used for stretch in wall to wall carpet, area rugs, floor mats, and wall art work.

CARPET CARVING

With carpet carving, designs are carved into the nap of the carpet with a carving tool.

A carving tool is a lot like an electric hair trimmer only much more powerful.

Carpet carving can be used alone or in combination with other custom carpet design methods.

CUSTOM RUG MAKING

To make area rugs you use various methods, like installing borders, inlays, and carpet carving. You could use one or multiple methods when custom carpet designing.

The seams and inlay patch work that shows on the back of the rug, are all covered with an area rug backing. A spray adhesive is applied to the back of the carpet and a new backing is applied.

The edges of the area rug are bound or surged with a binding or surging machine. The simplest rugs are made by only binding or surging around the edges. Binding the edge of the carpet refers to using a piece of fabric material sewn or stapled to the edge, while surging the edge sews colored thread around the edge.

CUSTOM CARPET DESIGNING

With custom carpet design **not only are you installing the carpet and stretching it through out the house, but, you are making the carpet as well.**

To do this you use rug making methods, like installing borders, inlays, and carpet carving. You could use one or multiple methods when custom carpet designing.

Inlays can be made to run around the entire perimeter of the carpeted areas. An example of this would be flowers and vines going around the living room, through the hall, and around the bedroom. Carpet carving is often also used to add details to the inlays.

Carpet carving can be used alone or along with other design methods. You carve designs into the carpet with carpet carving tools. A carpet carver looks like an electric hair trimmer.

NATIONAL EQUIPMENT, Inc.

National Equipment sells tools for rug making, inlays, carpet carving, and binding machines. They also have a rug making class.

www.nationalequipment.com
1-800-245-0267

CARDER INDUSTRIES, Inc.

Carder Industries sells tools for rug making, inlays, and offer a custom inlay/border package that includes a video tape.
1-800-323-RUGS

ADVERSE WEATHER CONDITIONS

Unless you live in a climate that has perfect weather conditions, you will be forced to work in snow, rain and cold conditions.

When carrying in carpet and supplies in snow and ice be very careful of your footing. It will be a struggle not to track in snow onto the new carpet. Try to get everything you need inside to minimize trips out to the van. Also, keep some scraps by the front door to wipe your feet.

In cold conditions the carpet becomes very

stiff, so give it some time inside to warm up before you try to stretch it.

In rainy wet conditions keep the carpet that is sticking out of the van covered with plastic.

Indoor room temperature should never be less than 65%

REPAIRS

The most common carpet repairs are carpet pulling out of pin metals, and patching carpet stains, burns, and holes, or cuts in the carpet.

Carpet pulls out of pin metals for a variety of reasons:

√ The carpet is incorrectly cut and not installed into the metal lip deeply enough.

√ A low grade pin metal that is to narrow, and flimsy was used.

√ The metal was installed incorrectly, it is angled downward so that the carpet will not hold into the metal.

√ The metal was not nailed firmly enough causing the metal its self to come loose.

√ The carpet is stretched excessively tight causing the carpet to pull out of the metal.

√ The carpet is poorly constructed and delaminating (the secondary backing coming loose).

REPAIRING CARPET THAT IS PULLED OUT OF A METAL

Remove the carpet from the metal to asses the cause of the problem. Repair the carpet backing with latex. Install a heavy weight pin metal correctly. Install the new metal in closer to the carpet so that the torn area of carpet is cut off. Restretch the carpet into the metal, cutting off the bad area.

If the carpet is torn back to far to restretch into a pin metal than you will need to use a flat bar metal nailed over the top.

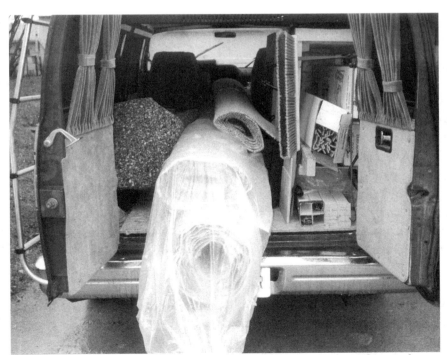

Keep the carpet covered with plastic during transpertation from the warehouse to the job site in wet conditions.

REPAIRING STAINS, TEARS, AND BURNS

Patching carpet stains and burns are a very common carpet repairs. They can be caused by a lot of things: burns, spilled sodas or juice, or pets digging into the carpet .

Repairing stains is done by cutting out the bad area and patching in with a piece of the same carpet. When cutting out a stain, cut out the smallest area possible, the smaller the cut out is the less the patch will show. A large cut out will almost always show. A cookie cutter is a tool that cuts a circle in the carpet for patching.

The old carpet you are repairing is often faded, and the patch piece that was saved in the basement is often like new. It may not look the same color no matter what you do. If you do not have a scrap piece of carpet for repairs you can often cut out a piece of carpet in the back of the closet to use for patching.

Place seam tape under the cut out and cut a new piece to fit in. Use a hot melt glue gun to seam it in.

Cleaning a stain may also be effective, purchase a cleaner for the type of spill that occurred and try scrubbing it.

If to large of an area of the carpet is damaged, I would not attempt to cut and patch it. It would be best to replace the whole area, because patches will most likely show excessively.

If a large area of carpet in the center of the room is damaged you may be able to do an inlay. This is done with a different type of carpet to create a custom carpet.

SEAM WELD IRONS

I talked about seam welding in the seaming section but would like to mention more about seam weld irons. Seam welding is the process of attaching the cut backing edges back together with a hot melt adhesive bonding the backings and yarn fibers. This eliminates the need to latex the cut carpet edges. A seam that is seam welded will not open up as much when bent and prevent seam peaking when the carpet is stretched. It also prevents any fraying of the pile yarn.

This is also approved to replace latexing the cut edges of the carpet. If a seam were inspected by a carpet mill a latex black light test would not be used.

Seam welding can be done with a hot melt glue gun by applying thermal glue to the cut carpet edges and then hot melt seaming. Using a hot melt glue gun is a longer and more difficult process. But by using a seam weld iron that applies adhesive to the cut edge while hot melt seaming, both are done at the same time and this is much more efficient. The adhesive is applied only to the backing and not on the carpet pile.

Seam weld irons are available from Taylor Tools. These high quality irons have a 24' cord and a thermostat that maintains an even temperature. They also have temperature settings that tell you the exact temperature of the iron, unlike most other irons.

TAYLOR TOOLS
11075 47th ave.
Denver, CO 80239
303-371-7667
Fax: 303-371-7669
web: www.taylortools.com

QUIZ - SECTION 5
Some Other Situations

1 T / F Wrapping carpet over ledges with railings to cut and go around have been a huge problem area with installers using carpets with low dense naps.

2 T / F It is a good idea to have two people working for carpeting walls.

3 T / F The original carpet in a trailer home often is turned under and stapled along the walls. Some trailers have the walls built over the top of the carpet.

4 T / F Carpet is installed on walls using

carpet nails,

5 T / F Toe kicks are the riser under kitchen cabinets and bathroom vanities.

6 T / F Sometimes, in a kitchen, bathroom, or commercial area, the whole perimeter of the room is cove based with carpet up the lower walls, instead of using vinyl cove base or wood base board.

7 T / F When the base board is being installed it should be raised 1 inch off of the floor. This allows extra space for the carpet to tuck and makes a smoother edge along the wall.

8 T / F You always have the perfect conditions, and **all times the base board are installed raised off the floor.**

9 T / F Borders are when a different carpet is seamed around the perimeter of the room.

10 T / F Borders can be used for stretch in wall to wall carpet, or be used in making area rugs.

11 T / F The width of the border depends on the size of the area that you are carpeting, and the look that you want to achieve. But always make the border at least 2' wide.

12 T / F Inlays are seamed in place from the back of the carpet, and a scrim is placed over the seams.

13 T / F For doing inlays a power cutter is used to cut out custom inlays, it cuts through two layers of carpet. This tool makes cutting inlays very fast and accurate.

14 T / F There are pattern designs available that are used with an overhead projector to project on to the backing of the carpet. This is used for doing borders in carpet.

15 T / F A carpet carver is used to carve custom designs in carpet.

16 T / F A spray adhesive is applied to the back of the carpet and a new backing is applied. This is done when making any border.

17 T / F Inlays can be made to run around the entire perimeter of the carpeted areas. An example of this would be flowers and vines going around the living room, through the hall, and around the bedroom.

18 T / F You carve designs into the carpet with carpet carving tools. A carpet carver looks like an electric hair trimmer.

19 T / F In cold conditions the carpet becomes very stiff, so give it some time inside to warm up before you try to stretch it.

20 T / F In rainy wet conditions keep the carpet that is sticking out of the van uncovered without plastic.

21 T / F National Equipment sells tools for rug making, inlays, carpet carving, and binding machines. They also have a rug making class.

22 T / F The most common carpet repairs are carpet pulling out of pin metals, and patching carpet stains, burns, and holes or cuts in the carpet.

23 T / F When cutting out a stain, cut out the smallest area possible, the smaller the cut out is the less the patch will show.

ANSWERS
1. T   2. T   3. T   4. F   5. T   6. T   7. F
8. F   9. T   10. T   11. F   12. T   13. T
14. T   15. T   16. F   17. T   18. T   19. T   20. F
21. T   22. T   23. T

SECTION 6
NON - STRETCHABLE CARPETS

What makes a carpet non - stretchable? A non - stretchable carpet has a type of backing that does not allow it to be power stretched over a carpet padding and hooked on to tack strip. So, the type of backing determines if a carpet is stretchable or not.

Kanga back and enhancer backed carpets are carpets with backings that would tear if you tried to stretch them with a power stretcher.

There are also two main types of non - stretchable carpets. These are **non - stretchable carpets - That do not wrinkle** and **wrinklable non - stretchable carpets**.

Some carpets are designed to be able to **loose lay**, **perimeter glue**, **perimeter staple**, or installed with a **double stick tape,** *with out wrinkling.*

Other non - stretchable carpets must be installed using a **full spread direct glue installation** method, *to keep them from wrinkling.*

TYPES OF NON - STRETCHABLE CARPETS - THAT DO NOT WRINKLE

KANGA BACK CARPET - kanga back carpet is also known as foam back or rubber backed carpet. The pad is already attached to this carpet. Not to be stretched.

ENHANCER BACKED CARPET - Has a pad attached to the back of the carpet. Installed the same as a kanga back carpet. Not to be stretched.

PVC BACKED CARPET - Has a heavy black backing, good for commercial carpet installations. Not to be stretched.

CARPET MODULE TILES - These are square tiles made of carpet. Not to be stretched.

INSTALLATION METHODS FOR NON - STRETCHABLE CARPETS - THAT DO NOT WRINKLE

Five methods of installation for non - stretchable carpets that do not wrinkle are: **direct glue full spread installation, perimeter glue installation , double stick tape installation, loose lay installation,** and **perimeter stapling installation**.

The procedures for all of these installations are similar to the procedures for direct-glue full spread installation, except for **carpet modules tiles,** which are explained later. (Refer to section 3 for a detailed outline of direct-glue full spread installation.)

Always check with the carpet manufactured when in doubt of the installation method.

LOOSE LAY INSTALLATION - Carpet is not attached to the floor in any way, it is loose laid and trimmed to the wall.

FULL SPREAD DIRECT GLUE - Carpet is glued directly to the floor. The entire floor is covered with adhesive using a trowel. The carpet is laid back in to the adhesive and rolled to bond to the floor.

PERIMETER GLUE INSTALLATION - Adhesive is spread only along the outside perimeter of the room and on seams, unlike a full spread installation where the entire floor is glued.

DOUBLE STICK TAPE - Double stick tape is used to hold the carpet in place around the perimeter of the room and on seams.

PERIMETER STAPLE - Carpet is stapled around the perimeter of the room to keep in place.

TYPES OF WRINKLABLE NON - STRETCHABLE CARPETS

These carpets will wrinkle if they **are not** installed using a **full spread direct glue** installation.

Always check with the carpet manufactured when in doubt of the installation method.

UNITARY BACKED CARPET - Carpet is back coated with a heavy latex, may or may not have a secondary action backing. Is a very stiff carpet. Preferred installation method is a full spread direct glue. May also be installed using a double glue installation. Some manufactures may indicate that these can be stretched, but this is not recommended. Must be rolled a second time 3 - 12 hours later.

CARPETS WITHOUT BACKINGS -

Outdoor carpets often have no secondary backing and can only be installed in a direct glue method.

There are also indoor carpets that have no secondary backing and should only be installed in a direct glue method.

INSTALLATION METHODS FOR WRINKLABLE NON - STRETCHABLE CARPETS

FULL SPREAD DIRECT GLUE - Adhesive is applied to the entire floor. The carpet is laid back into the adhesive to adhere to the floor.

DOUBLE GLUE INSTALLATION - A specialized padding is glued to the floor first, then the carpet is glued to the padding. Any carpet with a pre - attached padding would not be double glued. Roll with the lightest roller possible and still achieve a 50/50 transfer of adhesive.

√ *Always use an adhesive specifically intended for the installation of carpet.*

KANGA BACK & ENHANCER BACKED CARPETS INSTALLATION

Kanga Backed and enhancer backed carpets have a foam pre - attached to the backing of the carpet.

They are excellent for do-it your- selfer applications. They are less technical to install as they do not require stretching, and also do not require pad installation. This is the perfect situation for beginning to learn the installation techniques. The padding is already attached so that no pad installation is required.

Make sure that **the floor is clean and dry** as outlined under glue down carpet installations, section 3.

Lay the carpet out as you want it to lay when it's finished. Make very sure that it's laid with enough carpet through any doorways. You can butt the carpet up against a straight wall and eliminate the need to trim that wall if the wall is perfectly straight. Do not do this if it causes a seam in a doorway.

If there is to be a seam, cut the pieces for the seam with a top cut row cutter or straight edge. Cut one inch off of the edge of the main carpet to be seamed. Lay the seam together to make sure of the proper fit. You will use a seam seal adhesive along the cut edge of the seam.

If you have chosen to glue the entire carpet (full spread installation), then fold back one side and glue. I recommend using a release adhesive to facilitate removal of the carpet. Use weights to hold the carpet in place when folding it back. Adhesive buckets and tool boxes can be used for weight. Allow the adhesive to become tacky before laying the carpet back into the adhesive. Roll that side for proper contact.

Fold back the other side laying the seam pieces along the other wall ready to lay into place (this is if the seam is narrow and the seam pieces are small enough that you can move the seam pieces). Glue and roll the other side.

Apply a seam seal adhesive for direct glue installations to the cut edge of the carpet. Set the seam pieces into place.

You can **use the knee kicker to adjust the**

carpet into place.

Roll the area thoroughly with a carpet roller, so that 50% adhesive is on the floor and 50% to the carpet backing.

To trim the carpet use a tuck knife and crease the carpet along the wall. A good crease ensures a straight even trim. Top cut using your carpet knife. **Or use a wall trimmer for glue down installations**.

To **perimeter glue** or **tape** the carpet down, you fold back the carpet along all of the walls. Make very certain that the carpet does not shift out of place when folding it back. Tool boxes or glue buckets can be used to hold it in place.

If there is a seam, mark the area with a marker so that you can apply tape or glue there. Tape or glue around the entire perimeter of the room next to the walls. Allow the adhesive to become tacky before laying the carpet back into the adhesive.

Trim a perimeter glue and perimeter tape installation as you would for a direct glue installation. There is a **glue down trimmer** that can be used although most installers simply use a knife. Make sure to have plenty of sharp blades when top trimming. Use the knee kicker to pull out any wrinkles.

To **perimeter staple**, you need to have a gilli gun stapler. You do not need to fold back the carpet for this application. The staples are narrow so that they do not show as much as a large staple. You only staple around the perimeter near the walls. Use the knee kicker to remove any wrinkles as you are stapling. Trim as you would for the previous installations.

OUTDOOR CARPETS

Ensure that **the carpet is for outside use**. These areas are exposed to extreme weather conditions.

Next **ensure that the adhesive purchased is for outdoor installation. A solvent based carpet adhesive** is preferred for outside installation. If a latex adhesive is used make sure that it is formulated for outside use.

Do not attempt to install over brick or slate. Any excessively rough surface should not be installed over. The surface should be clean and dry. Areas around swimming pools should not be used during installation and not for 24 hours after installation. Indoor pools need to be ventilated to lower the humidity and enhance the drying.

Check the weather forecast, to time the installation for a dry period of at least 24 hours.

Outdoor carpets should be rolled with a roller for the correct bond. The weight of the roller should be no more than 75 lbs. A substitute roller is your tool box tray. Use a steel tray and test it for snagging before proceeding. Grip the handle and place all of your upper body weight on the tray sliding it across the carpet. Start in the center and work your way outward systematically.

OUTDOOR CARPET SITUATIONS

- ◆ Concrete and wood patios
- ◆ Concrete steps
- ◆ Wood steps
- ◆ Wood decks
- ◆ Five season porches
- ◆ Screened Porches
- ◆ Sun decks
- ◆ Swimming pool areas
- ◆ Boats
- ◆ Entry ways

CARPET MODULES (TILES)

Carpet modules are also known as carpet tiles generally come in 18 x 18 inch squares with and with out pad.

They can be installed by **taping**, **gluing** or **stapling**. They are installed unlike any other carpet. When installing make sure to butt all edges up evenly and tightly. Carpet tiles are perfect for do-it yourself installers. Make sure that the floor is clean as in other direct glue situations.

TRUE / FALSE QUIZ
SEC 6
NON - STRETCHABLE CARPETS

1. T / F Kanga back carpets are installed using a power stretcher?

2. T / F All non - stretchable carpets must be installed using a full spread direct glue installation?

3. T / F Non stretchable carpets have a type of backing that can not be power stretched?

4. T / F Some non - stretchable carpets are non - wrinklable and can be installed using other methods rather than a full spread direct glue method.

5. T / F A kanga backed carpet can be installed using a loose lay method with out wrinkling.

6. T / F Carpet Module Tiles are always stretched.

7. T / F A **solvent based carpet adhesive** is preferred for outside installation.

8. T / F Always check with the carpet manufacturer when in doubt of the installation method.

9. T / F To **perimeter staple**, you need to have a gilli gun stapler. You do not need to fold back the carpet for this application.

10. T / F Trim a perimeter glue and perimeter tape installation, as you would for a direct glue installation.

11. T / F A carpet with no backing will wrinkle if it is loose laid, perimeter stapled or perimeter glued.

12. T / F What makes a carpet non - stretchable? A non stretchable carpet has a type of backing that does not allow it to be power stretched over a carpet padding and hooked onto tackstrip. So, the type of backing determines if a carpet is stretchable or not.

13. T / F There are two main types of non - stretchable carpets. These are **non - wrinklable non - stretchable carpets** and **wrinklable non - stretchable carpets**.

14. T / F Some carpets are designed to be able to **loose lay**, **perimeter glue**, **perimeter staple**, or installed with a **double stick tape,** *with out wrinkling.*

15. T / F Five methods of installation for non - wrinklable non -stretchable carpets are: **direct glue full spread installation, perimeter glue installation , double stick tape installation, loose lay installation,** and **perimeter stapling installation**.

16. T / F Outdoor carpets often have no secondary backing and can only be installed in a direct glue method.

17. T / F An enhancer backed and kanga backed carpet can be installed using a double glue installation.

ANSWERS - Non - stretchable carpets
1. F   2. F   3. T   4. T   5. T   6. F
7. T   8. T   9. T   10. T   11. T   12. T
13. T   14. T   15. T   16. T   17. F

APPENDIX

OTHER PUBLICATIONS

FLOOR FOCUS
914-764-0556
Fax - 914-764-0560
www.floorfocus.com

FLOOR COVERING INSTALLER MAGAZINE
Floor covering installer magazine is an excellent educational source for carpet installers. It is a quarterly publication.
22801 Ventura Blvd. #115
Woodland Hills CA 91364
818-224-8035
fax 818-224-8042
www.fcimag.com

FLOOR COVERING NEWS
516-932-7860
Fax - 516-932-7639
www.floorcoveringnews.com

NATIONAL FLOOR TRENDS
248-362-3700
Fax - 248-362-0317
www.subscribeforfree.com

FLOOR COVERING WEEKLY
516-227-1342
Fax -516-229-3600
www.floorcoveringweekly.com

The CFI PROFESSIONAL
Americas Monthly Floorcovering Installation Newspaper
Published by the International Certified Floor Covering Installers Association.
CFI
2400 East Truman rd.
Kansas City, Missouri 64127
1-816-231-4646
www.cfiinstallers.com

CLASSES & SCHOOLS

INTERNATIONAL CERTIFIED FLOORCOVERING INSTALLERS ASSOCIATION INC. (CFI)
The CFI offers certifications for both residential and commercial installation from level I - Masters certification. The certification is a two part hands on test and written exam. You must have two years of installation experience before qualifying for this certification. They also have a two day course for estimating and measuring, and a course for becoming an installation inspector. The CFI holds a yearly convention with seminars, networking, and exhibitors.
CFI
2400 East Truman rd.
Kansas City, Missouri
64127
1-816-231-4646
www.cfiinstallers.com

ORCON TOOL COMPANY
Orcon is a manufacturer of high quality floor Covering installation tools, they also produce a series of carpet seaming tapes that are very educational and entertaining. Orcon offers training at class rooms and hands on installation areas.
1-800-41ORCON or 1-800-416-7266
www.orcon.com
For more information on Orcon, and it's tools and products call:
1-800-227-0505

THE CARPET AND RUG INSTITUTE (CRI)
The CRI is the national trade association representing the carpet industry, the organization's membership includes manufactures of carpet produced in the United States and suppliers of raw materials and services to the

industry. They publish a wide variety of booklets and videos. They publish the study materials used for the **International Certified Floor Installers Certification**, *CRI 104 standard for installation of commercial carpet* and *CRI 105 residential installation standard.*

THE CARPET AND RUG INSTITUTE
Box 2048
Dalton, Georgia 30722-2048
706-278-3176
www.carpet-rug.com

NATIONAL CARPET EQUIPMENT

These hands on training courses cover all phases of rug design, carpet carving, sculpting, bas-relief, binding, hand tufting, fiber optic, shop set up, custom computer designs, marketing, bidding, equipment use and maintenance. Students become members of the National Association of Rug Makers and Sculptors (NARMS).
1-800-245-0267
www.nationalequipment.com

FLOOR COVERING INSTALLATION CONTRACTORS ASSOCIATION

FCICA was officially incorporated in 1982. They were formed by the Carpet and Rug Institute to advance the installation industry, developing standards of installation, and educational material. They hold yearly conventions offering educational seminar classes, networking, and also offer the Floor Covering Training (FIT) program to provide installation training.

FLOOR COVERING INSTALLATION CONTRACTORS ASSOCIATION

FCICA
7439 Millwood Drive
West Bloomfield, MI 48322
248-661-5015
877-TO-FCICA
Website: www.fcica.com
email: info@fcica.com

VERMONT CUSTOM RUG COMPANY

Offers a Woven carpet training book that includes a chapter on hand sewing.

David Hunt
18 Burpee Road
Bristol, Vermont 05443

OTHER ORGANIZATIONS & COMPANIES

CRAIN CUTTER CO. INC.

Crain is a manufacturer of high quality floor covering installation tools and supplies. Contact Crain for a floor covering supply distributor in your area. Crain offers complete training clinics it various distributors locations.

CRAIN CUTTER CO. INC.
156 South Milpitas blvd.
Milpitas, CA 95035 -5459
1-408-946-6100

ROBERTS CONSOLIDATED INDUSTRIES, INC.

Roberts is a top floor covering tool and supply manufacturer. Contact them for a floor covering supply distributor in your area.
1-800-423-6545
Fax - 1-800-423-6544
www.roberts-consolidated.com

OPERATIONAL SAFETY AND HEALTH ADMINISTRATION (OSHA)

OSHA is an office of the federal government that over sees and sets regulations for safe working conditions. Failure to comply to the regulations can result in fines. Find out more on their web site at:
www.osha.gov

MOHAWK INDUSTRIES

A carpet manufacturing mill located in Dalton, GA.
1-800-241-4900
706-272-4902
Fax: 706-272-4800
web: www.mohawkind.com

SHAW INDUSTRIES

A carpet manufacturing mill located in Dalton, GA.

706-275-1700
Fax:706-275-1719

THE ENVIRONMENTAL PROTEC-TION AGENCY (EPA)

The EPA is an office of the Federal Government that over sees environmental issues in the U.S.A.. It allows the floor manufacturers to place its (Indoor Air Quality) green label on carpet backing, showing compliance with air safety standards. The impact of dumping huge amounts of synthetic carpet and pad in land fills is unknown, previously most carpet was produced with natural fibers. Contamination of the soil and water could result. Most pad is now being recycled into new pad, yet a good use for recycled carpet has not been found. Find out more on their web site at:

www.epa.gov

The WORLD FLOOR COVERING ASSOCIATION

The WFCA hold a **floor covering installation open** competition each year. They offer installation training classes (the RITE® Program) in carpet, hardwood, laminate, and ceramic flooring installation at the Anaheim, CA head quarters, and through out the U.S.A.. Time is split between presentation and hand on work. Each class includes an exam. The program concludes with a presentation of certificates. The WFCA also offers Virtual Campus classes and Certifications for business owners and managers, administrative people, and salespersons. The WFCA holds an annual educational conference. They offer many other benefits for its members, including discounted car rentals. You may become a members to this fine organization and receive its many benefits

.World Floor Covering Association
2211 East Howell ave.
Anaheim, CA 92806-6009
800-624-6880
714-978-6440
email: wfca@wfca.org
www.wfca.org

ENVIROMENTAL GROUPS

Caliber Publications supports these enviromental groups and companies:

The AMAZON CONSERVATION Team
Mark J. Plotkin, Ph.D.
4211 N. Fairfax Dr.
Arlington, VA 22203
Tel: 703-522-4684
Fax: 703-522-4464
Web: www.amazonteam.org
email: mplotkin@amazonteam.org

CO-OP AMERICA
National Green Pages
1612 K Street NW, Suite 600
Washington DC 20077-2573
Tel: 800-58-GREEN
Web: www.coopamerica.org

Publishes a nation wide directory of products and services for enviromental people and from enviromental businesses.

DEFENDERS OF WILDLIFE
1101 Fourteenth St., N.W., RM. 1400
Washington D.C. 20005
Web: www.defenders.or
www.kidsplanet.org
Tel: 202-224-3121

EARTH TONES
the Enviromental Telephone Co.
1530 Blake St., Ste. 220
Dever Co 80202
Tel: 888-327-8486
Web: www.earth-tones.com
Email: jwhite@sharegroup.com

The only long-distance company to give 100% of its profits to environmental groups. Low business, residential and calling card rates. Bills on recycled paper with updates on enviromental issues.

ENVIROMENTAL WORKING GROUP
www.ewg.org

THE WORLD FLOOR COVERING ASSOCIATION
FLOOR COVERING COMPETITION

Have you ever thought about competing in floor covering Installation competitions? The World Floor Covering Association has a competition each year. Regional competitions are held each year across America , each regional winner then competes in the nationals at Las Vegas, NV.

Eric Larson placed 5th in the Midwest in the **2001 WFCA Carpet Installation Competition.** Skills must be displayed in borders, inlays, hand sewing, steps, as well as knowledge in carpet manufacturing construction. A written test is taken and then followed by the hands on competition.

PESTICIDES EXPOSURE AND THE
CARPET INSTALLER

In 1989, farm worker's Union leader Cesar Chavez went on a hunger strike, to protest the exposure of his members to the carcinogenic chemicals used on grapes. The health hazards from pesticide exposure had been almost completely over looked in the case of carpet installers. Pesticides are a known carcinogen, cancer causing substance.

Carpet installers are at a high risk of exposure to pesticides when removing old carpet and gripping it along the walls. They are at a high risk when working along the wall boards and floor around the perimeter of the room, as is done when installing tack strip and repairing old tack strip. They are also at risk when reinstalling used carpet and when restretching carpet.

Pesticides are applied along the wall boards and floor of the room, just where carpet installers do a lot of their work. Apartments use routine maintenance programs, applying pesticides every three to four months. When a tenant moves out a thorough treatment is applied, either on top of the old floor covering or after the carpet is removed. Residential homes also use pesticides on a routine maintenance basis.

Pesticides are not regulated in most states and can be purchased by anyone at the home and yard departments of many stores. This makes the application even more dangerous when applied excessively, and incorrectly by an untrained person.

In 2001 New York state passed laws to protect citizens, children and home owners, from the pesticide spraying of others. Requiring anyone using these products to place advanced warnings.

On May 26, 1998, John Van De Camp, Attorney General of California, plus public citizen, the Natural Resource Defence Council, sued the EPA for its failure to protect us from carcinogens. The law suite listed seven carcinogenic pesticides that are still in wide spread use: benomyl, trifluralin, phosmet, chlordimeform, mancozeb, dichlorvos, and dicofal.

Carpet installers are virtually never informed of these pesticide applications and customers don't think of this danger. Installers must be made aware of this health hazard and customers must be required to disclose the history of home and commercial pesticide treatments prior to any installation.

Installers need to be warned of this danger so they can protect themselves. Wear protective rubber or latex gloves when removing carpet or working in any area that has had pesticide treatments. Require all disclosure of pesticide use in any area you will be working in and wear protective clothing.

References:
Dr. Michael Colgan, 1990 Colgan Institute of Nutrition, Prevent Cancer Now
Dr. Matthis Rath, M.D., 2001, Cancer, Cellular Health Series
Brian Lavendol, Ted Williams, Audubon, Sept. - Oct 2001, Taking back the halls, Out of control

The Carpet Installation Training Handbook

THE FUTURE OF CARPET INSTALLATION

The price carpet installers are receiving for their services has not increased with inflation for the majority of installers. While plumbers, electricians, heating and cooling companies and general contractors are making enough to take regular vacations, own retirement accounts, (Sep and roth IRA'S) and quit by 5:00 each evening to relax and spend time with their friends and families, carpet installers are, installing that extra night job and still struggling to pay the bills!

There are no government regulations with floor covering installation as there are with plumbers and electricians. The government agencies don't see any dangers in floor covering, as they do with other trades, so, any one can become a floor covering installer with little or no training. And there is no apprenticeship program that must be followed. There are also next to no Union with floor covering installers as there are with other trades. Many salesmen and customers feel that the cheaper the installation the better.

Carpet installers don't run their businesses, they allow carpet stores to run their businesses! Carpet stores tell the installers how much they will be paid for the job and the installers are expected to take what they get, even if it means they have to install tack strip on concrete for half the day, free!

While other trades run their own businesses and advertise for their services, they bid their own jobs, they have their businesses computerized so they know exactly how much they are making, or loosing, at any time in a given month and they definitely do not work for half the day free because a salesman bid the job for them. With out even looking at it!

It's not the fault of carpet stores and it's not the fault of salesmen, it is the fault of the **carpet installers.** Installers must further their education in business, they must continue to further their floor covering skills and they must run their own business. Carpet installers should run phone book ads for their business and they should advertise their services in newspapers. When the customer calls you directly you can go measure the job and *bid it for what you are worth*! Installers must be payed extra for installing concrete tack strip, they must be paid extra for steps, and they should also be paid extra for seams!

Unfortunately not all installers are worth the same price. An installer who is Master II Certified with over 10 years of experience and a member of the Better Business Bureau, is worth much more than an installer who trained for one year, then went on his own. Apprenticeship programs must become mandatory, requiring a minimum of three years as an apprentice, if not four.

Although some installers don't believe in Unions, but they have worked very well for other trades. A Union would, standardize prices with union installers with the same skills, negotiate prices with stores and organize strikes if negotiations are not worked out. All Union members would be required to be Certified with the International Certified Floorcovering Installers Association (CFI), or World Floor Covering Association, follow an apprenticeship program and guarantee that their installers are experienced and educated.

The future of Carpet installers is up to the **installers** themselves. They will either become better business men or go out of business and I don't believe that "carpet" in its self will go out of style in the near future, styles will change of course, but their will always be carpet, for a long, long time to come.

ABOUT THE AUTHOR

Eric Larson began working in the carpet installation business in 1991. He started as an apprentice, training with several quality installers and over a two year period developed the skills to begin his own business. Eric is the owner of Caliber Floors, a carpet installation business.

He is a writer and self publisher and is the owner of Caliber Publications. He is the author of three books on carpet installation, *The Carpet Installation Training Handbook*, *Measuring for Carpet and How Did Carpet Get In This House any way?*

Eric is a member of the *International Certified Floorcovering Installers Association* and is certified through Residential II and Commercial II. He competes in the (WFCA) World Floor Covering Association, Carpet Installation Competitions.

Eric is not a one dimensional person and has many hobbies. He enjoys spending his spare time listening to live music and spending time outdoors mountain biking and hiking.

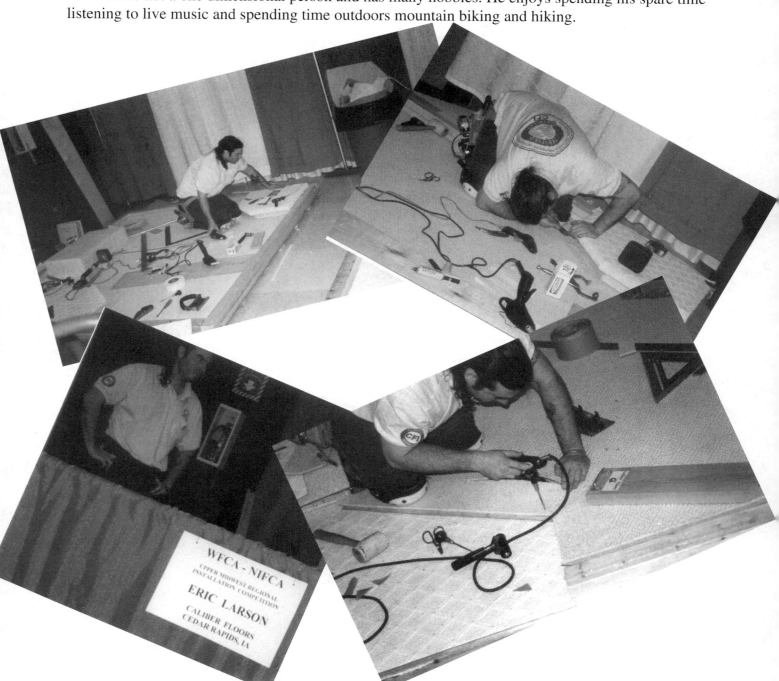

SELECT REFERENCES:

1. The Carpet and Rug Institutes, CRI 104, 1996 Standard for Installation of Commercial Floor Covering Materials.

2. The Carpet and Rug Institutes, CRI 105, 1995 Standard for Installation of Residential Floor Covering Materials.

3. David Hunt, Woven Training Study Guide, Vermont Custom Rug Company

4. David Hunt., Hand Sewing, chapter 7, Vermont Custom Rug Company, Woven Training Study Guide

5. The CRI Carpet and Rug Institute, Carpet and Your Indoor Environment, 2000

6. The CRI Carpet and Rug Institute, Indoor Air Quality Testing Programs.

7. CRI Carpet and Rug Institute, Carpet and Indoor Air Quality in Commercial Installations, 1994

8. Floor Focus, www.floorfocus.com

9. FLOOR COVERING INSTALLER MAGAZINE

10. FLOOR COVERING NEWS

11. NATIONAL FLOOR TRENDS

12. FLOOR COVERING WEEKLY

13. The CFI PROFESSIONAL, Americas Monthly Floorcovering Installation Newspaper

14. INTERNATIONAL CERTIFIED FLOORCOVERING INSTALLERS ASSOCIATION INC. (CFI), certification study guides.

15. ORCON TOOL COMPANY, series of carpet seaming tapes

16. NATIONAL CARPET EQUIPMENT, carpet carving, binders, surgers, and inlay tools.

17. The World Floor Covering Association, installation competition testing.

18. Carder Industries, Inc. custom carpet instructional video tapes.

19. Occupational Safety and Health Administration, codes of federal regulations, Labor part 1926, 1998.

20. Environment Protection Agency, (EPA) Department of the federal government.

21. CFI Convention, 2001 Anaheim, CA, • **Seminars and Workshops -** Woven Workshop by David Hunt, Backings ! Backings ! Backings ! By Doug Amundson and Jon Namba, Beveling - Binding - Borders - Creative Rug Making by Tim Carder of Carder Carpets and Dave Edwards, Hand Sewing - Power stretching - Stair Upholstery Workshop by Fred Chastain.

22. (FCICA) FLOOR COVERING INSTALLATION CONTRACTORS ASSOCIATION

Index

WHAT INSTALLERS ARE SAYING?

Eric's Dedication to actively support the floor covering industry is admirable. I would like to commend Eric for his effort to improve several areas of this industry. I hope this book will be widely read and well received, spawning a renewed interest in the education of "Professional" floor covering installers.

Tom Miller - Manager of Hanks Specialties Cedar Rapids, IA. Tom began installing carpet in 1982. Tom has been a National Board Member of The International Certified Floorcovering Installers Association (CFI). He was the Local Cedar Rapids, IA Chapter President of the CFI from 1996 - 2002. He is also a technical advisor for the Carpet Installation Training Handbook and listed under the technical advisory board in this book.

I have been installing carpet since 1992 and over the years I have gained most of my knowledge by going to different schools. This book has everything in it that I learned in the schools, at a fraction of the cost. For the do-it-your-selfer it is the ideal book to read.

Jim Pawledge - DBA Competitive Flooring, Cedar Rapids, IA

This book is useful for the basic training of new apprentices and for a reference book for all sales people dealing with customer problem jobs

Dick Wessels - DBA Wessels Floor Covering, Cedar Rapids, IA. Dick is a Master certified installer with the (CFI) and was the chapter president for many years. He is also a technical advisor for the Carpet Installation Training Handbook and listed under the technical advisory board in this book. He began installing carpet in 1973 and owned a retail floor covering store.

I very much enjoyed reading the book. This not only taught me a few new techniques but also was a good source for polishing up on some traditional methods of installing. This was a very easy book to read and gave very thorough explanations and instructions. I believe this book will not only be good for newcomers to our profession but for veterans as well. There is no one in this business who couldn't benefit in one or more ways from reading the Carpet Installation Training Handbook.

Jason T. Gloede - DBA Gloede Vinyl Installations. Jason started installing in 1995 and currently works at Hanks Specialties in floor covering supply distribution. He is still installing on the side. He has completed Armstrong vinyl school, as well as Shaw carpet school.

This book is written so that most people can understand the details of carpet installation and the illustrations enhance the written portion of the book. I believe, the carpet installer is thought of as a second class tradesman and until apprenticeship is reinstated I do not believe it will change. Installers should be licensed and trained in money management as well as other business practices. This book is a good start in the right direction.

Carol G. Hayek - CFI Master Installer # 1688, past president of the Cedar Rapids, IA CFI chapter. Carol has been installing since1963 and trained for three years as a Union apprentice. He has owned the Carpet Chalet, INC. in Cedar Rapids, IA since 1969 and not only sells carpet but still is installing carpet. He is Armstrong and Domco trained in vinyl, Shaw trained in soft back and experienced at hand sewing woven goods.

INSTALLER PROFILE INTERVIEW

Date: 7-9-1998
Name: Anthony C. Katch (Tony) - Cover Model and pictured through out the Carpet Installation Training Handbook. Tony runs a quality floor covering business in Cedar Rapids, IA.
Age: 26
In Business: Since 1990

How did you get started in the floor covering business? I started part time with an installer to learn the skills of installation.

What do you like most about the carpet business? The satisfaction of the quality job I've done and the pay!

What do you like least? The pressure of being to busy.

What advise would you give to someone wanting to get into the business? **Just Do It!!!**